YOUR FINANCIAL COACH

COACHING YOU THROUGH
THE HIGHS AND LOWS
OF A PRO SPORTS CAREER
– AND MAKING IT ALL
COUNT FINANCIALLY.

Your
FINANCIAL
C⚽ACH

PRACTICAL FINANCIAL AND LIFE ADVICE FOR PROFESSIONAL SPORTSPEOPLE

DARREN BAKER

Matador
9 Priory Business Park
Kibworth Beauchamp
Leicestershire LE8 0RX, UK
Tel: (+44) 116 279 2299
Fax: (+44) 116 279 2277
Email: books@troubador.co.uk
Web: www.troubador.co.uk/matador

ISBN 978 1780882 055

British Library Cataloguing in Publication Data.
A catalogue record for this book is available from the British Library.

Typeset in Adobe Garamond by Troubador Publishing Ltd

Matador is an imprint of Troubador Publishing Ltd

DISCLAIMER

This book is intended as general information on becoming personally and financially organised now and for the rest of your life. Everyone's circumstances are different and what is right for one person may not be suitable for another. Before taking any action you should seek the advice of a qualified financial planner, legal adviser or accountant.

ACKNOWLEDGEMENTS

A great many people helped me with this book. I am extremely grateful to every single one of them for their encouragement, generosity, time, support and words of wisdom.

Particular thanks go to:

Adam, Adrian, Alan, Alistair, Andrew, Andy, Anita, Arul, Ben, Bo, Bob, Charlotte, Charlie, Chloe, Claire, Dave, Dawn, David, Dean, Derek, Godfrey, Gordon, Greg, Guy, Jasmine, Jason, Jeni, Jens, Jerard, Jessica, JJ, John, Kevin, Kim, Laura, Marcus, Martin, Max, Nadeem, Neil, Nik, Pat, Paul, Phil, Richard, Ronnie, Tony, Sally, Sarah, Sean, Shaun, Shauna, Sheila, Steve, Stuart, Terry, Tim, Tom, Victoria, Vicky, Will and Zara.

CONTENTS

PROLOGUE

There's nothing quite like the life of the sports professional.

Waking up every morning and earning your living from doing something you are passionate about is a rare and privileged position to be in.

But it can be a precarious existence – a bit like walking a tightrope. Just one bad injury away from the final whistle; or one good performance away from the headlines.

Many elite athletes do find themselves having to retire early – usually as a result of injury. And it is at that low point they are deposited back into the "real world"; sometimes without the qualifications or experience required to compete for skilled jobs.

Importantly, even if you are lucky enough to have a long and successful career, you are still likely to retire at a relatively early age – what then?

Andre Agassi

"The problem with athletics is that you spend a third of your life not preparing for the other two thirds."

My reason for writing this book is to provide busy professionals – men and women with perhaps very little time, or interest, in doing anything other than their chosen vocation – with a succinct guide to the important issues that they really must get to grips with.

The core of the book deals with Financial Management – how to go about organising and managing your monetary affairs. Because whatever you might think about the effectiveness or morality of our capitalist society, money is one of the most important subjects in our lives.

I also consider other common challenges that many sports people face during their careers – and offer a summary of the counsel I've collated from professionals, past and present, and others involved in the sporting world.

Whatever stage you might be at in your professional career, my hope is that by highlighting these issues and providing some practical tips and advice, I can minimise anxiety, cut down on prevarication and spur you into taking some positive action.

My aim is to help you make the most out of this momentous time in your life, whilst also setting yourself up for the next phase.

Good luck and best wishes,

Darren Baker

INTRODUCTION

So – you've made it.

The training, the hard work, the sweat, and the tears –
it's all paid off. You've arrived – the dream has come true
– you're a professional sportsperson.

You might think the really tough stuff is pretty much behind you now – you've
put in the hours, done the legwork and certainly had your setbacks and
successes along the way. But now your face fits. You may even have got the car,
the property, the recognition – and perhaps think that as long as you stay fit
now and don't do anything silly, it'll all be fine.

But you'd be wrong. Success means that everything gets more complicated.
Serious stuff – money, contracts, sponsorship, insurance, agents, tax bills.
Things you might not know much about – but you know you should.

In the back of your mind – although you probably don't like to admit it – you know that this might not last forever – or even for very long. It's tough at the top and it's a fickle world. Just one bad injury could put paid to all this. So you want to make sure you make the most of what you have right now. And make plans for the future. Right now.

To compete at the highest levels these days takes more than talent alone – you need an unbelievable level of passion, determination and dedication. Whilst most people will understand that competitive urge, very few possess the skill, courage and devotion necessary to fully rise to the challenge.

However, whilst you might possess a mental discipline that helps you excel at your chosen sport, this same, almost blinkered mind-set can often mean that other areas of your life are neglected – and usually your finances are pretty low down on the list of priorities.

Ignoring the financial realities of life however, can have devastating consequences. You need to be pragmatic. You need to look ahead every now and again and not just focus on the here and now. You need to plan.

Robert G. Allen

"Money is one of the most important subjects of your entire life. Some of life's greatest enjoyments and most of life's greatest disappointments stem from your decisions about money. Whether you experience great peace of mind or constant anxiety will depend on getting your finances under control."

Think…

You probably know people that have made good choices – a retired pro? … and achieved happiness and financial security.

Similarly, you may know some people that have made bad decisions; or who haven't planned properly …and are now struggling both emotionally and financially.

This book contains powerful lessons

Over the last year I have spoken to many professionals, both current and retired, from the UK and abroad – and from numerous sporting disciplines. I also talked with coaches, agents, managers, psychologists, lawyers, physios and other support specialists to improve my understanding of the journey sports professionals go through – how they deal with the huge highs and lows that are a part of their unique way of life – and how they feel about money management.

The levels of personal and professional success varied but there were clearly shared issues and challenges. Patterns quickly emerged and it became obvious that there were common reasons why some people struggled emotionally and financially, whilst others flourished.

My research also showed that, whilst financial reward is not a top priority for most professional sports people, in the end (especially post retirement), just like the rest of us, their financial health has a huge bearing on the quality of their lives and on their emotional well-being – the two are inextricably linked.

It was clear that there were lessons to be learnt but that the support and guidance on offer was patchy and sometimes inadequate. So, I thought it would be of value if I wrote this book – in the hope that by sharing this collective experience and expertise, more people might enjoy greater whole life security.

I have written the book in a particular order for a good reason. Hopefully it will become obvious as you read it.

Each chapter covers one key stage that you need to address – and includes helpful check and to-do lists that summarise the vital issues; as well as the action you need to take.

But you can also dip in and out whenever you need information about a specific issue or topic – making it the ideal handbook to keep in your kit bag.

Importantly, the book poses lots of questions – many you should ask yourself and some you need to ask your advisers. These questions are designed to get you thinking about what it is that you want to achieve and the steps that you need to take to get there. Hopefully this will motivate you into taking action.

The book is split into three main sections, which follow **my simple financial training method.**

Preparation

Getting your head around this significant time in your life – helping you work out what you want to achieve – and getting to grips with the current state of your finances. Why it is important to plan for your future and how understanding a little about the psychology of money will help you embrace good financial habits and avoid making costly mistakes.

Training

Structure and process – why you need a "plan" and how to go about putting one together. The issues you need to consider – and choosing who you are going to trust to help you.

I have added a separate section on "Investing" as this is such an important, but complex subject.

Performance

When it really counts. Developing a healthy approach to managing your life and managing your money – and making it all work for you.

Marshall Goldsmith

"What got you here, won't get you there."

If you follow all of the recommendations in this book you will significantly increase your chances of achieving success – success being very much a personal reality, but one that I simply define as "being able to afford to be happy."

Like any coach however, I cannot guarantee you success. I can only point out the things you should be doing and draw your attention to some of the common mistakes and bad habits that will damage you – both financially – and because the two are intrinsically linked – emotionally.

You are ultimately accountable – you cannot completely delegate your responsibilities to someone else. The most important thing you can do now is realise how important these issues are and start addressing them.

Yes, getting some professional help will probably be a good idea and securing the right coaches can make all the difference. But taking time to understand the journey that is ahead of you – and educating yourself – will undoubtedly be one of the most important investments you ever make.

By following the steps set out in this book you will understand the issues and the factors that can affect your decision making – which will enable you to make informed decisions. By taking positive action you will improve your chances of achieving long-term financial security – and from that position of strength, you will enjoy greater personal choice and freedom.

CHAPTER ONE

PREPARATION

As with sport, a basic rule applies when managing money – you don't decide that you are going to do something and then just jump right in and try and do it.

At best you might get lucky and do a passable job, but you could also do more damage than good.

If you are really going to get your finances in order then you need to think about what this involves and how you are going to go about doing it.

I appreciate creating your own financial plan from scratch can feel like a daunting task. The good news is that you don't have to do it all at once. And, if you follow my plan you will quickly see some tangible benefits which will help spur you on to the next stage.

"PPPPPP"

Proper Preparation Prevents Pretty Poor Performance.

What we cover in this chapter:

1. Why being young can be a disadvantage.

2. A big question – one that all professional sportspeople have to face at some point. Possibly a pivotal moment or an on-going means of motivation.

3. Why proper financial management is so important and how you can motivate yourself when it comes to dealing with money.

4. The preparation work you need to do before you can start to build a Financial Plan; starting with how to get a clear picture of where you stand financially right now.

5. Setting aims and goals – what it is that you want out of your life, both now and in the future – and what role does money play in helping you achieve those goals?

6. Through a little self-awareness and by using some simple planning techniques, how you can make budgeting much easier and dramatically improve your money management skills.

7. The psychology of money. How your good and bad money habits can have a huge impact on your level of financial success.

8. Money and relationships – keeping your emotions from clouding your judgement.

9. A few issues to consider if you are lucky enough to be earning a lot of money.

WHY BEING YOUNG CAN BE A HANDICAP

Young people sometimes find it difficult to relate to their peers; which can make the transference of knowledge and experience problematic.

Oscar Wilde

> *"When I was young I thought that money was the most important thing in life; now that I am old I know that it is."*

The problem can be one of seemingly different values and beliefs – having little in common. It doesn't help that we just aren't genetically hard-wired to want to pay attention to older people – when we are young we have an absolute in-built belief that we are right and in charge, so what's the point?

> *"Solipsism". The belief that the only thing somebody can be sure of is that he or she exists, and that true knowledge of anything else is impossible.*

Many young people show solipsistic tendencies. This is not meant as a criticism. Solipsism is in a sense the default state of humanity – a personal trait that we are all inherently born with and only lose gradually over time as we gain more experience about how the world works.

When we are younger the kernel of us believes, perhaps only subconsciously, that we are the only thing that really exists and that nothing else matters. That feeling we have – certainly that behaviour we exhibit – of utter selfishness as a child, absolutely demanding, transfigures into the common adolescent intuition that we are invulnerable, almost marked out for something special, but in any event simply not capable of dying, not in our present gloriously fresh state of youthful supremacy.

Now you may, understandably, be reading this and thinking "what the heck is this guy talking about? And how does this have anything to do with me?"

But if you think about it – this unqualified self-belief and feeling of invincibility is a huge, in fact essential, quality for a young athlete to have – or any young person for that matter. You need to be selfish and totally focused if you are to stand any chance of achieving your goals.

But this insular attitude and instinctive indifference to anything outside your own sphere of existence can make it very hard for you to appreciate the relevance and value of the older generation's experience. A bit like the frustrated parent trying to get their kids to listen, whilst all they want is for them to stop interrupting their exciting lives with some boring story from the "good old days."

Andy Caddick, Somerset and England Cricketer

"Be a sponge – learn from others. The best players absorb everything, have the guts to try different/new things, and figure out what works best for them. Don't discard anything, regardless of whether you think it is relevant at this moment or not. Take it all on board as it will probably be relevant at some point."

You are indeed special, but you are also a flesh and blood human being who has to make their way in this, the real world – and we oldies do have a lot of useful information that can help you make the most of your life. Yes, we aren't as young, fit, strong, well-trained or good looking as most of you (well, not any more), but we do have something of real value to offer.

All we ask is that, even if you don't always see the immediate relevance, you listen to what we have to say, and think about how you might be able to use that information to your advantage.

"By the time I realised the value of my parents' advice, I had made all of the same mistakes they had – plus a few new ones of my own."

ARE YOU REALLY UP TO THE REQUIRED STANDARD?

This might seem like a negative question – but it is a valid one nonetheless. It just depends on the context in which you ask it.

If you are in the early stages of your sports career; perhaps still contemplating whether you should pursue (or continue to pursue), this lifestyle choice; then you certainly need to ask yourself – "Am I really good enough?"

Paul Reed, European Pro Tour Golfer

"Get as much advice and information as you can – on whether you are really good enough to make it; what the life is really like; and how to best go about getting from where you are now, to where you want to be."

By "good enough" I don't just mean do you have the talent and dedication; although that is obviously part of it. But in the context of this financial management book, I am particularly asking whether your talent, properly nurtured, can generate sufficient income to support an acceptable level of lifestyle?

You may well have already answered this question to your own satisfaction – if so, great. But if you haven't, then you might want to think about it. Because in a world where fractions of a second often mean the difference between first and last, "almost good enough" can also mean the difference between a healthy and an empty bank account.

Most hopefuls will never succeed in making the huge leap from amateur to professional – finding that they are just not good enough to compete consistently at the top level. Many pros will spend years trying to improve, only to finally accept that it is not to be – having achieved some level of success, but a long way short of what they had hoped for and certainly not enough to make a decent living out of it.

It is only the small number at the top of each sport who will be good enough, or marketable enough, to attract sufficient money (wages, funding, sponsorship, endorsement etc.) to be able to support themselves without having to rely on getting money from elsewhere e.g. funding, second job, partner, parents.

Now, I am not saying that you shouldn't try just because the financial rewards might not be there – far from it. Of course no-one should ever give up just because they might never top their field, or only earn enough to scrape by – competing, not winning, is what sport is all about after all. I am just saying that many young people dream about a life in professional sports without really appreciating how tough it is to compete at that level, or what the financial realities are likely to be for someone with their level of talent.

Bo Eason – NFL Houston Oilers, now Broadway Playwright, Actor and International Speaker

"Don't waste your opportunity – stay with it and finish what you started. There is a huge difference in outcome between giving 100% effort and commitment and just doing enough."

If you simply love what you do and neither the level of sporting or financial success you achieve is an issue – then you are truly a lucky person. A happy, fulfilled life is, after all, everyone's ultimate goal.

But you need to be honest about where your sporting skills are likely to take you and the journey that lies ahead of you. Are you are really prepared to make the huge sacrifices that your lifestyle choice is going to demand? Do you know what the financial reality of that lifestyle is likely to be and is that a monetary existence that is i) Feasible? ii) Acceptable?

Can I be good enough? And what do I need to do in order to get better e.g. what coaching and resources do I need?

What is likely to be my financial position if I do pursue my sporting career? Will I have to rely on the support of other people? If so, are they willing to support me, and if so, for how long?

How will my financial position change if my career progresses as I (realistically) hope it will? What kind of lifestyle will this give me?

Or, should I perhaps stay amateur; earn a living doing something else and enjoy my sport part-time?

And, remember, it is unlikely to be just you making sacrifices – very few people achieve success without enormous support (time, energy, money, accommodation), from a whole host of devoted people – parents, partners, coaching staff etc. If nothing else, you owe it to them to ask yourself these questions – and to discuss these issues with them.

A positive motivator

Even if the question of your career choice is moot, it does not mean that this question is invalid.

Every sports person I interviewed was highly driven – determined to be the very best they possibly could. But what I noticed was that the very top athletes/players had something extra – they didn't just want to be the best they could – they wanted to be the best – "full stop."

Andy Caddick, Somerset and England Cricketer

"Give 100% and if you still feel you can give a little more – then give it. The last thing you want to do is look back and wish you'd done that bit more."

And part of how they become "the best" was by measuring their own performance against that of their peers.

By continually assessing what their fellow players/competitors were doing – by constantly asking "Am I really good enough?" – they were always looking for ways to learn, ways to improve and thus stay ahead of the competition. As a result, they consistently performed to the very best of their ability and did indeed become "the best of the best."

WHY IS PROPER FINANCIAL MANAGEMENT SO IMPORTANT?

I started this book with Robert G Allen's quote because for me it perfectly sums up why it is so important to get our finances under control – the quality of our lives, to a significant degree, depends upon the condition of our finances.

William Somerset Maugham

> *"Money is like a sixth sense – and you can't make use of the other five without it."*

With finance, as in sport, proper preparation is vital if you want to maximise your level of success.

Japanese Proverb

> *"Planning without action is futile; action without planning is fatal."*

Before you even start thinking about money, you need to start by getting your head around this significant time in your life – work out where you are – what you want to achieve both personally and professionally – and then you can start to plan on how you are going to make it happen.

Whilst your talent may be special and what you do as a sportsperson sets you apart – you are not immune to the everyday demands and realities of modern life.

All of us endure an emotional roller-coaster ride as good times and not-so-good times come and go. Money is regularly quoted as one of the main reasons why people are stressed and also for relationship breakdowns. Why? Because money is emotional.

And the fact is that money worries are not confined to those who don't quite have enough of it. Whatever your net worth, you have the same basic concerns –

to protect your financial security and preserve your standard of living. And in my experience those who have gone from little to lots often feel that pressure most keenly.

And financial stress is exacerbated by uncertainty and unpredictability – two unavoidable aspects of a professional sportsperson's life. Whilst many talented men and women scrape by on modest wages or funding, only the very small minority generate large incomes – and even then the irregularity and unpredictability of their earnings can be a significant issue.

Of course, non-performance income e.g. sponsorship, endorsement and appearance fees can dramatically, and very suddenly, change your financial reality. That one good, high-profile performance can change everything, but this is only ever going to be true for a relatively small number of people; and often only for a limited period.

The lack or unpredictability of income can be used as an excuse not to think about, let alone plan, one's finances. Of course, these issues make things a bit more challenging but that is no excuse not to plan at all – in fact it is exactly the reason why proper planning is even more important.

PLANNING TO SUCCEED

Here's another famous quote. Whilst you might say: "Doh! Of course I have to live within my means", and you do; it is not always simple to achieve in real life.

Charles Dickens

"Annual income twenty pounds, annual expenditure nineteen pounds, nineteen and sixpence (£19.96), result happiness. Annual income twenty pounds, annual expenditure twenty pounds ought and six (£20.06), result misery."

If you don't know where you currently stand then this is the first thing you need to correct. But you also need to have some idea of what money means to you and of what you want your future life to look like – because your chances of actually getting there are greatly reduced if you don't. And even if you do make it, or fail along the way, how will you know?

You need a plan that has clearly defined goals, a realistic timetable and a clear method of how you are going to achieve success. Only then are you going to be in a position to make good decisions and avoid making costly mistakes.

And a big bonus that you will get from planning this way is "peace of mind." Knowing where you are financially – that you have planned properly – and that you have done all you can to protect your future, is immensely reassuring.

HOW TO MOTIVATE YOURSELF WHEN IT COMES TO MONEY

Whilst we all have to deal with money – very few people enjoy it.

Many find money a mystery – often frightening. A lack of knowledge and familiarity, about what can often be highly complex subjects, can create a serious lack of confidence.

Our education system in this country doesn't do a particularly good job preparing us for the financial realities of life – even the simplest money management is rarely taught in school. And the finance profession doesn't help matters with its fanatical obsession with jargon, which can make even simple matters seem opaque or impenetrable. Parents can have a big influence on our attitude to money – but not always in a good way.

When it comes right down to it, we all need to have a reason for doing something – especially if we don't want to do it. Often it is either the stick or the carrot and with money I find using both works rather well.

Without control over your money, and therefore your life, you are enslaved to those who understand it.

Later in this chapter we consider what money does for you – the life that it allows you to live. We explore the various phases of the life ahead of you; and get you thinking about what you might want that life to be like. Finally, we contemplate what would happen if you didn't achieve your goals. What would be the implications? And how would this make you feel?

Your personal goals are just dreams with a deadline (and often a price tag).

Goal setting is important – what better motivation than working towards the achievement of one's aspirations? As professional athletes, you appreciate that in order to achieve your objectives you need to plan properly and execute that plan diligently.

It helps if you have clear, objective information, presented in a way you can easily evaluate. You can then see the benefits that planning will deliver and appreciate the potential consequences of not doing it.

Getting organised does take some time and effort, but stick with it and you will quickly start to reap the rewards. Don't try and tackle it all at once – prioritise and deal with one issue at a time.

"How do you eat an elephant?
One bite at a time."

You can't just jump from A-Z anyway. You need to build a financial plan one step at a time – starting with the basics and adding more information and knowledge gradually. Don't jump ahead of yourself as it is unlikely to make sense.

TAKING CONTROL

It is time to confront reality. You need to know where you currently stand financially and whether your situation is good, indifferent or bad – and you need to know this before you can move on.

If your finances are shared with a partner – a husband, wife or "significant other" – this should be a joint exercise.

Tracking your money flow

You need to be clear as to how much net (i.e. after tax) income you have coming in and how much expenditure you have going out.

Whilst most people will have a pretty good idea of what their income is, some only have a vague idea about how much they spend and what they spend it on – in my experience there are often a few surprises when it's analysed.

Keith Davis

"We didn't actually overspend our budget. The allocation simply fell short of our expenditure."

Whilst you don't have to budget down to the penny, a reasonably precise summary of your income and expenditure is a vital first building block in your Financial Plan. If this bit isn't accurate then all of the subsequent planning work will be flawed.

So, get out your bank statements and credit card statements and look at everything you have spent in the last 12 months. Then fill out the income chart and spending charts overleaf.

You want to work out the monthly average for each category. If your earnings are irregular then add up last year's total and divide by twelve. If there has been a major change in your "regular" income and you can be sure this change will continue in the future e.g. pay rise, qualified for funding, or lost sponsorship then use this amended figure going forward. For less secure income e.g. bonuses, sponsorship or endorsement income then make as good an estimate as you can – but it is always better to under-estimate income than over-estimate it, and vice-versa for expenditure.

For bills paid annually or at irregular intervals then divide the total paid in the last year by twelve.

Be Realistic

You must be realistic. With financial planning a bit of pessimism (even though I really don't like pessimists), is healthier than over-confidence.

When projecting future income always be as accurate as you can be but err on the side of caution – do likewise for your expenditure. Better by far to have a bit more in the bank than you expected than to not have enough because you over-estimated your bonuses, or under-estimated your outgoings.

YOUR INCOME

HOW MUCH DO YOU EARN EACH MONTH?

Salary (take home)   £ _____

Funding   £ _____

Endorsement/Sponsorship   £ _____

Appearance fees etc.   £ _____

Bonuses   £ _____

Earnings of partner (take home)   £ _____

State benefits   £ _____

Maintenance or child support   £ _____

Investment income   £ _____

Rental income   £ _____

Other income (specify)   £ _____

TOTAL NET INCOME   £ _____

download

You can download this and many other useful resourses by visiting our "toolkit section" at **www.yourfinancialcoach.co.uk/toolkits**

YOUR EXPENDITURE

When analysing your expenditure you need to split your out-goings into "fixed" costs and "discretionary" costs?

A fixed cost is one that you simply cannot avoid – food, "basic" clothing, mortgage/rental payments, taxes, utility costs, car insurance etc. However, just because you can't avoid them doesn't mean that you cannot reduce these costs e.g. by shopping around, using comparison websites, paying utility bills on-line (when in addition to helping you budget, you can also ensure they don't build-up high balances in their favour that you could better use yourself.)

A discretionary cost is one that you don't have to incur but choose to because it adds something to your life e.g. holidays, designer clothes, eating out, theatre trips, a "nice" car. Discretionary costs can be reduced or even eliminated if you have to.

Now obviously everyone will have their own opinions as to what is necessary and what is not – and the amount of money that is reasonable to spend on each item. But you need to be realistic, pragmatic and sensible when considering what you can spend in relation to your available net income.

And what about cash withdrawals that you use to cover those small expenses? These can really add up. Do you draw a lot of cash? If so, what do you actually spend it all on? Perhaps try carrying around a small notebook to make a list of all those little things you buy – you might be surprised just what you spend and on what.

FIXED EXPENSES

HOME

Mortgage/Rent	£
Electricity	£
Gas	£
Water rates	£
Council Tax	£
Service charge	£
Buildings insurance	£
Contents insurance	£
Other (specify)	£

TRANSPORT

Car loan	£
Car maintenance	£
Fuel	£
Car insurance	£
Road tax	£
Public transport	£
Taxis	£
Other (specify)	£

REGULAR EXPENSES

Food	£
Cleaning and toiletries	£
Laundry	£
Medical costs	£
Other (specify)	£

DEBT REPAYMENT

Home	£
Student loans	£
Credit cards (min.)	£
Store cards (min.)	£
Personal or bank loans	£
Other (specify)	£

OTHER BILLS

Agent's fees	£
Telephone – fixed	£
Telephone – mobile	£
Childcare/maintenance	£
Other (specify)	£

INSURANCE AND SAVINGS

Life	£
Income protection	£
Private health	£
Critical illness	£
Pension	£
Mortgage endowments	£
Other (specify	£

TOTAL FIXED EXPENSES £

DISCRETIONARY SPENDING

ENTERTAINMENT		IRREGULAR EXPENSES	
Restaurants/Takeaways	£	Home repairs	£
Pub, Off licence	£	Appliances	£
Tobacco	£	Car servicing & repairs	£
TV	£	Pets inc. vet bills	£
Internet	£	Holidays, travel	£
Books, magazines, papers	£	Christmas	£
Music	£	Birthdays	£
Cinema, concerts, theatre	£	Other gifts	£
Hobbies	£	Charitable donations	£
Club memberships	£	Clothing	£
Kid's activities	£	Toys	£
Gambling	£	Hairdresser	£
DIY	£	Other beauty treatments	£
Gardening	£	Other (specify)	£
Other (specify)	£		

TOTAL DISCRETIONARY SPENDING   £

TOTAL EXPENDITURE (FIXED & DISCRETIONARY) £

download

You can download this and many other useful resources by visiting our "toolkit section" at www.yourfinancialcoach.co.uk/toolkits

PRIORITISING YOUR DISCRETIONARY SPENDING

Financial planning is all about making the most of a limited resource – money. To do that you not only need to split your discretionary from your fixed expenditure, but you also need to prioritise it.

Charles A Jaffe

"It's not your salary that makes you rich, it's your spending habits."

Consider how much enjoyment, benefit, and/or value you really get from each discretionary pound that you spend?

Use the table on the next page to rank each item in its order of importance to you. I have given you some descriptions below to help you, but have left them purposefully generic as personal interpretation here is important. But be honest with yourself – especially when it comes to what is and what isn't really a fixed cost.

Think about what items you would spend more money on – if you had more money. And, importantly, consider which items you would cut back on first if your income went down.

Basic living expenses – food (basic not luxuries), electricity, gas, mortgage, fuel, clothing (reasonable) etc. – the costs you incur just to maintain a basic level of existence. Not much you can do about most of these apart from ensure you are paying a competitive price. But it is incredibly easy to spend a lot more than you need to at the supermarket, or on take-away meals –remember this is discretionary spending.

Cars – realistically what do your cars cost? Not just in fuel, maintenance, insurance etc. – but in depreciation. You will have to replace them at some point, so when and how much is this likely to cost? Even if you get a car as some sort of endorsement/sponsorship deal, the likelihood is that you will have to pay tax on the "benefit in kind" you enjoy as a result. This may be deducted automatically from your wages but it is still a cost that you need to include in your budget, and what would happen if this benefit was no-longer available to you?

Have you perhaps decided to buy a "nice" car – one with a prestige badge, or lots of expensive extras? If so, then the additional cost of this car over and above that of a "reasonable" car is discretionary spending. I appreciate this is a subjective calculation, but my point stands.

Enhanced lifestyle priority 1 – what do you spend on those little extras, that make life easier and/or more enjoyable, but aren't strictly essential? E.g. dining out, designer clothes, hobbies, theatre etc.

Enhanced lifestyle priority 2 – what else do you spend on things that really, really aren't necessary, but you like them? And after all, you can afford them e.g. school fees, first/business class travel etc.

Travel – you may be able to split your travel into various sections – some more important e.g. work, the annual family holiday (fixed and/or discretionary), with others if time and finances allow? (definitely discretionary).

Gifts – annual birthday and Christmas gifts, weddings, house deposits for the kids – all these regular and future costs need to be considered.

Big bonus wish list – do you have other things that you want to do – your bucket list – if and when time and finances allow? E.g. round the world trip, buy a boat, start a business?

DISCRETIONARY EXPENDITURE – DESCRIPTION & PRIORITY

PRIORITY	CATEGORY	DESCRIPTION	FIXED EXPENDITURE £	DISCRETIONARY EXPENDITURE £	FREQUENCY
1	Basic Living Costs				
2	Enhanced Lifestyle 1				
3	Enhanced Lifestyle 2				
4	Cars (basic)				
5	Cars (enhanced)				
6	Travel				
7	Gifts				
8	Bucket List				

These are my Financial Objectives as agreed in priority order.

Name _____ Date _____

download

Download this resourse by visiting our "toolkit section" at www.yourfinancialcoach.co.uk/toolkits

PUTTING DISCRETIONARY SPENDING INTO CONTEXT

As I have pointed out previously, discretionary expenditure is anything you spend money on that is not an essential expense. But there is nothing wrong with spending your money on things that make you happy – assuming that is, you can afford to do so.

But what a lot of people find very difficult is knowing how they should be balancing their current discretionary expenditure with the "right" amount of saving towards things they might want in the future. After all, it is very easy to spend the money we have today, and enjoy the benefits, but not so easy to put that money aside to fund something that might be years off – especially if those goals are still undefined.

Have a look again at the current totals of your net income and total (fixed + discretionary) outgoings. Then look down your list of discretionary spending and think about each item.

- How much of your total net income do you currently save?
- Do you think the split between spending and saving is reasonable – really?
- Are *you* really getting maximum value from each £ you spend?

You don't necessarily have to come up with definitive answers at this stage – although you might identify a few areas that you now want to work on.

What I am trying to do by asking these sorts of questions is make you aware of the fact that money is very personal and that, in the end, it's only you who can decide how best to utilise the financial resources you have. But you must also realise that if you choose not to manage your money effectively then you are likely to waste some of it – and that will mean it won't be available for you to spend on things you want in the future.

We look at how much you should save, and how to get into the savings habit, later in this chapter.

STOP AND THINK FOR A SECOND

One of the most dangerous stages in our financial lives is when our income increases – especially when that extra cash is not required to fund our fixed costs.

Some people's first tendency when they get some money is to spend it. The sirens of commercialism call with promises about making you beautiful and sexy – or providing you with prestige and status – or making your life better. And of course, you work extremely hard so why shouldn't you enjoy the fruits of your labour?

Bo Derek

"Whoever said money can't buy happiness simply didn't know where to go shopping."

The problem is that spending can become habitual and it is very easy to get into the routine of automatically looking for something to spend any excess cash on. But you haven't got an unlimited supply of money so when you spend some on X, you will no longer be able to afford Y. You need to ask yourself: "Is this a good trade-off?" "When the bill arrives, will your life have really improved or have you mistaken a short-term material buzz for something more profound?"

So, if you are lucky enough to benefit from some extra cash, think carefully before you simply look for something to spend it on. Often what not to spend is just as important as what to spend your money on. And remember, you probably owe 20/40/50% to the taxman!

You might not feel any pressure whilst you are focusing on your career – especially if you are earning good money. But at some point your sporting income will start to fall and it is usually at this point you realise that the cost of maintaining your existing lifestyle is not affordable. Don't be one of those people who think of all the things they bought which they now wish they hadn't.

YOUR BALANCE SHEET

Next you need a simple document that summarises your current wealth.

Use the balance sheet overleaf to list your assets and your current liabilities – the difference between the two is your net worth.

When listing the value of your assets, be realistic. Put down what you would get if you sold, or cashed them in tomorrow, not what you hope you might get if sale conditions were perfect. For many assets the figure is likely to be a lot less than you might want it to be.

Make a note by the side of each debt showing when the next payment is due, what interest rate you are paying (or would be paying if you don't repay the debt e.g. credit card), and the amount of any early repayment penalties if you were to repay it, or some of it, before the stipulated time. On some debts e.g. personal loans, you might be able to repay more than the minimum usual amount without incurring any penalty or charge.

Whilst it is very easy to extend our spending power with credit, it all has to be repaid at some point. Knowing which debts are costing you the most to service enables you to target your repayment strategy efficiently.

Paying off a debt is generally better financially than having interest on savings e.g. interest payment on credit card 15%, savings rate 1.5%.

YOUR BALANCE SHEET

ASSETS		DEBTS		DATE DUE	INTEREST RATE
Cash in current accounts	£ _____	Mortgage	£ _____		
Cash in savings accounts	£ _____	Student loans	£ _____		
ISAs	£ _____	Credit cards	£ _____		
Endowment policies	£ _____	Store cards	£ _____		
Pension schemes	£ _____	Catalogue/mail order	£ _____		
Life/Illness insurance	£ _____	In-store credit	£ _____		
Property	£ _____	Bank loans	£ _____		
Investments	£ _____	Friend/family loans	£ _____		
Car	£ _____	Unpaid bills	£ _____		
Jewellery	£ _____	Other debts (specify)	£ _____		
Antiques/collectables	£ _____				
Other (specify)	£ _____				
TOTAL ASSETS	£ _____	TOTAL DEBTS	£ _____		

download

You can download this and many other useful resources by visiting our "toolkit section" at www.yourfinancialcoach.co.uk/toolkits

INITIAL CONCLUSIONS?

What do the numbers tell you? Has your normal, monthly expenditure been more or less than your income?

Is there anything likely to happen in the future that could increase or decrease either your outgoings or your income so that the current dynamic changes? Is this very likely to happen, or do you just hope/fear that it will happen? Be realistic.

What about your expenditure? Can you make some easy savings by cutting out, slimming down, or by shopping around e.g. using comparison websites?

Thomas Jefferson

"Never spend your money before you have it."

What about the relationship between your "regular" income and your "regular" bills? If you rely on irregular income to help pay your monthly expenditure then you need to ensure that you manage this relationship properly. There is no point getting a bill which needs paying this month that you can't pay until you get your next round of funding, endorsement or appearance money. Don't spend future income and ensure you put aside some of your irregular income if you are going to rely on this to pay future bills.

Remember, most of us have a tendency to live to our means – effortlessly increasing our spending to match our income. It can be very easy to under-estimate what we spend; or write-off past "one-off" or "extra-ordinary" expenses on the basis that they are unlikely to happen again. Whilst that may indeed turn out to be the case, life does have a tendency to throw unforeseen costs at us, so it is often a good idea to include an element of unknown costs just to be on the safe side. Better to have money left over than not enough!

Think hard about where your discretionary spending goes. Most of us find it difficult to strike a reasonable balance between buying the things we like and putting sufficient aside to provide financial protection and fund our future goals. At least by ensuring you get personal satisfaction from every pound you spend means that you don't waste money.

But the main thing is that you now know where you currently stand financially and you will hopefully have some ideas on how you can improve things a bit. You can now work towards going from where you are to where you want to be.

MAKING LIFE EASIER – MONEY MANAGEMENT PROGRAMMES

You can make your financial life, especially budgeting, much easier by utilising technology.

Personally I use a computer programme into which I download bank statements via my on-line banking account. This is really easy to use and allows me to see exactly what I have spent my money on using the report feature.

Whilst you might think you know exactly how much you have spent and on what, your memory may not be as good as you think it is. Having the evidence presented to you in a report like this makes it very clear where it is all going. In my experience a lot of people are surprised just how much they spend and on what.

These programmes do have lots of other features which can help you keep track of debts, savings and help plan for future bills. But to be honest, even if you don't find these extra options of use, the core bank statement and reporting features are worth the relatively small cost of the programme itself.

If you are happy using on-line banking I would highly recommend getting one of these programmes. I understand some people are worried about security, but as long as you follow the protocols and keep your passwords and account numbers safe, there really shouldn't be an issue.

There are numerous good money management programmes on the market and most bank accounts now have a free, on-line accessibility option. Some banks even provide the money management programme itself. Why not take a look?

THE BIG QUESTIONS –
WHAT DOES MONEY MEAN TO YOU?

Take a moment and consider what your money currently does for you and how having enough of it helps make your life possible and even enjoyable. It:

- Enables you to pursue your sporting career.
- Permits you to afford a certain level of lifestyle.
- Provides some level of financial security.
- Gives you financial peace of mind.
- Possibly funds a few luxuries, a hobby, or passion.
- It might enable you to look after and provide for your family.

Now, probe a little deeper and ask yourself some questions about where you are in your life right now. The idea is to start identifying the things that you might want to achieve – the general issues that are important to you – and areas of financial weakness that you need to address.

Here are a few questions to get you started, but if you really think about it you will know what issues are important to your life.

Answer "yes", "no", or "I'm not sure."

- Are you completely satisfied with the way you manage your money? If not, why not?
- Are you happy with your current overall standard of living?
- Do you like where you live?
- Do you pay off all of your debts, in full, every month?
- Do you have enough put aside to fund those costly little emergencies e.g. car repairs, freezer breakdown etc. without having to give up something else?

- Do you have enough to fully support yourself for at least 3 months if you were to lose your income for some reason?
- Do you have sufficient savings and/or insurance to protect yourself and your family in the event of serious illness or injury?
- Are you putting enough away, and in the right places, to sustain your desired standard of living when you retire from sport, and then again when you finally retire from work?

When answering these questions, list what you like about your current position and also what you would like to change/improve.

If you answer "No" or "I'm not sure" then try and envisage what "Yes" would look like – that is your goal.

LOOKING TO THE FUTURE

An important part of financial planning is considering what you want your life to be like years from now. And now that you have some basic financial data at your finger-tips, you can start to explore what this might mean for you.

What do you want to get out of your life beyond sport?

Some people are striving for something, but are just not sure what. Others have never really thought about it. It seems only the lucky few know exactly what they want out of life, but even some of them haven't got a plan as to how they are going to turn their goals into reality.

Now, I appreciate that for some people this question, at least at the moment, may seem unimportant or even irrelevant. You may indeed have little interest in looking to the future – but that will change.

Even if you think that trying to plan for an as yet undefined future life is a futile exercise, hopefully you will at least concede that you will want certain things as you go through your life and that many of these will come with a price tag.

Whilst it may not feel like it, you are currently in just one phase of many that you will enjoy as you go through life. And, there will be things you want that at some stage you won't be able to have unless you plan in advance for them.

Have a think about how your life might unfold.

Starting out – low income (in my case spent entirely on having fun) and low responsibilities.

Spurs earned – income on the rise and you can now start to afford a few little luxuries – more fun, but also time to start thinking about money management and, in particular, getting into the savings habit.

Work peak – earning potential maximised and even with increased spending, income should still exceed expenditure. Time to consider bigger purchases e.g. car, house etc. but also time to take your financial planning seriously – and save more!

Family arrival – may still be earning well but current and future expenditure (and responsibilities) just went up dramatically! More planning issues to consider.

Career declining – peak performance period over and earnings may be on the wane. But expenditure unlikely to fall as you have gotten used to having a certain lifestyle. If you haven't already (and you really should have by now), then you need to get a plan in place for your life post sport.

Retire from sports – uncertain future employment and income prospects? Still want to maintain a good standard of living but can you afford it, and if so, for how long? This is when good money management during your playing career really pays off.

Post sports career(s) – possibly good short-term earnings potential using name/fame, but longer-term potential will probably depend on you acquiring new skills.

Retire completely – completely reliant on pension and savings to fund your lifestyle for the rest of life. Have you saved enough?

SETTING GOALS

Enabling you to make the most out of the opportunities available in each stage of your life is what Financial Planning is all about.

But as many of the things you will want in life come with a price tag, you will only be able to take advantage of them if you have sufficient money available. And as the cost of many items will exceed what you can afford from your normal, regular income, this means you need to save – often for years in advance.

Of course sacrificing now for an as yet undefined future cost is difficult. So the better the picture you can paint of what your life might look like, the easier it is to motivate yourself to start planning for it now.

Start by projecting yourself forward – not too far – say 2-3 years.

1. Think about what you would like your life to be like at that point – describe it.

2. What progress would you have to make, both personally and professionally, between now and then for you to be completely happy?

3. Write down each of your goals – describing them in detail so someone who doesn't know you could understand what it is that you are trying to achieve.

Failure
Now consider what would happen if you don't achieve your goals? What would be the implications? How would this make you feel?

Success

Finally think about what it would be like if you did achieve your goals. What would that do for you? What would be the implications? And how would this make you feel?

Now consider a little further ahead, say 4-7 years – and ask yourself the same questions.

Finally think about what you would want your life to be like 1-year after retiring as a sports professional.

I appreciate this can be a difficult exercise for some people – especially if you are young and find it hard to envisage anything beyond a few weeks/months, let alone a few years. But understanding the fundamental role your money will play in your life is crucial – money is, after all, just a means to an end.

Even if you don't know exactly what it is that you want from life, hopefully this exercise will at least open up your mind to the possibility (reality!) that your life will have multiple phases. And that at some point you will want things that cost money – probably lots of money and certainly more than you have right now e.g. home, car, family, your own business, retirement etc.

As in sports, you need to be emotionally engaged if you are to be motivated to put a plan in place that will give you the best chance of getting there. You then need to follow that plan.

What you do during your sporting years will likely affect your standard of living decades from now. Delay taking an interest and you may well find yourself unable to live the life you want and without the time left to correct things.

Sophie Tucker

"I've been rich and I've been poor: Rich is better."

Planning ahead is especially important for sports professionals because their earning life can be back to front – short, profitable career whilst you are relatively young – followed by a lengthy period of potentially much lower earnings – and then retirement.

And, as I have said before, don't be put off just because you can't visualise exactly what it is you are planning for. Very few people have a clear idea of where they want to be, or what they want to be doing 5, 10, 15 years from now – and anyway life has a knack of evolving so it is likely that even the best laid plans will change over time.

Clinton Jones

"I have never been in a situation where having money made it worse."

The important point is to recognise that managing our finances effectively is something we need to do – because if our finances are healthy we get to enjoy greater security and choice – which also means our lives are less stressful.

WHAT IS YOUR NUMBER?

If you know where you want to go and/or what you want to achieve, it is possible to "put a number" on the cost of achieving your goals.

Putting a price tag on your goals is important. Knowing what your aims and goals might cost allows you to join up the dots – from the life you have now to the one you hope to live. It firstly enables you to work out whether you are likely to be able to afford your aims/goals; and if so, how much you will need to earn and save in order to achieve them (and many people regularly under-estimate just how much they do need to save).

It might be more than just one number – one for each goal. It might be an income figure e.g. sufficient income to cover your future expenditure and/or a capital figure so you can finance something like a house purchase, wedding, school fees or business start-up.

Such future numbers are financial targets, not absolutes – the future, by definition, being unknown. But most people are comfortable enough with painting a picture of what they hope their future life will look like – and from that, what that future life is likely to cost.

Once you have your costs, which are likely to be present costs e.g. that house currently costs £250,000, you can apply a reasonable set of assumptions e.g. inflation will average X% per annum, and work out the future cost. You can then work backwards to calculate how much you need to save in order to accumulate that amount in the given timeframe.

I appreciate that all these calculations sound complex, and they can be, but this is the kind of thing a good adviser can help you with – many will use a cashflow programme that is specifically designed to do this kind of future planning – see the Lifetime Cashflow Programme in the Performance chapter.

Whatever your number, the likelihood is that it will probably change several times as you go through the various stages of your life. But as long as you have a structured financial plan in place then you will be able to see how this can be adapted to accommodate any changes.

GET INTO THE SAVINGS HABIT

Most people find it very easy to spend whatever level of money they may have coming in. After all, being able to pay your bills and have those little extras can make life easier and more enjoyable.

However, good financial management is all about getting into the right habits – and saving is one of the most important. You need to be realistic about the need to save and be sensible about how you go about doing it.

Most of us are creatures of habit and often the routine we get into is spending whatever income we generate. But if we want to be able to afford our goals we need to put some of our current income away to help fund them and the sooner we get into the custom of doing this, the easy it is to do – and the sooner we achieve our goals.

How much to save is a very difficult question. You obviously can't save if you really don't have any spare money left over each month, but it is rare to find someone who couldn't cut down their outgoings even a little bit to generate some money they could then put aside.

You need to be honest with yourself when you review your expenditure. Yes, finding some money to save might involve giving up, or reducing your spending on things you like doing but – as with all things in life – there has to be a balance.

If you can, I would try and save at least 10% of your net income. Although, if you have the capacity to save more then I recommend that you do so – one American ex-basketball player told me that the best bit of advice he was ever given when a player was "Spend 10% and save 90%."

But whatever the level of your earnings, the important thing is to get into the habit of saving and to do this early – almost something that you do automatically. If you have to think about what to save and then arrange this, more often than not you will find some reason not to do it.

One suggestion is to set-up a direct debit each month that transfers your chosen figure into a savings account. If you do it so that the funds leave your account as soon as they arrive e.g. pay day, then you will find that because you never had the money for long enough to miss it – you won't.

If you start saving early on then you will also find the habit much easier to adopt and maintain. Treat saving as you would every other expense and ensure you allocate it in your budget. You will quickly find that it becomes a part of your financial routine and an expense that you don't notice.

If your income goes up, immediately increase the amount you put into savings.

OK, you might want to enjoy some of your extra cash but be realistic and reasonable about the amount of extra funds you put away.

Saving is something you must do and the trick is to make it easy on yourself – habit, discipline and structure.

THE PSYCHOLOGY OF MONEY

Look back at the work you have done so far and consider what it says about you and your attitude towards money.

- Why do you currently spend the way you do?
- Are you satisfied with your debt management?
- How do you feel about the amount you are saving at the moment?
- Are you motivated to plan for the future, or do you just not see the point?

Whilst some people try and think of money as simply a solution to a practical problem – and in very simplistic terms it can be – the reality is that money is a very emotional subject. And because of this, our financial decision making can often be driven by psychological factors, rather than logic and evidence. Such decisions are sometimes neither rational, nor in our best interests.

It is important that you appreciate how your emotions can affect the way you go about managing money. Understanding this relationship will enable you to make better decisions and avoid making costly mistakes.

On the one hand, money is a positive influence in that it enables us to fulfil certain needs. The basis of Maslow's famous theory of motivation is that human beings are driven by unsatisfied needs – and that certain base needs e.g. physiological, safety, love, and esteem, must be satisfied before we can move up the scale and eventually achieve self-fulfilment.

The satisfaction of these needs is healthy – in fact it is essential to our well-being. Being unable to fulfil them will make us stressed, ill, act out of character, or even act immorally.

Maslow's Hierarchy of Needs

Money obviously can't solve all of your base needs but it goes a long way to enabling you to achieve some of them e.g. paying for your mortgage/rent, utility bills and food. Being financially secure undoubtedly delivers enormous psychological peace of mind; it enables you to get out and socialise, and can as a result, help you feel good about yourself. Conversely, being worried about money can be emotionally draining.

This basic relationship between money and our psychological well-being doesn't change when you acquire more money. Believe me, everyone's number one concern, whether rich or poor, is that one day they will find themselves unable to maintain their desired lifestyle.

But appreciating that good money management can be a positive force in your life does not mean that you will always make the right choices. Often we just don't know that we are sabotaging ourselves with the decisions we make. Sometimes, even though we know we are not doing the right thing, we concoct excuses to justify our actions and make them acceptable.

By understanding a little about why we act in the way that we do, we can identify personal traits that can potentially cause us harm – and once we know what these are, we can take action to ensure they don't adversely affect our decision making in the future.

WHAT IS YOUR FINANCIAL PERSONALITY TYPE?

Self-awareness will help you understand how your personality can affect your decision making, and as a result, why your finances are in the shape they are. This will help you get into good habits and cut out any bad ones.

Are you a gambler? Willing to ignore the risks to try and make that big score. Do you really understand the risks you are taking though? Have you over-estimated the upside and under-estimated the downside?

Are you an ostrich? For whatever reason you don't like, or don't want to deal with your finances, even if you know that there is a problem or an issue you really need to tackle. You would much rather ignore them completely even though you know this course of inaction will not end well.

Are you an excuse maker? You know you need to get things organised but there is always a good reason why you can't just now.

Are you a big spender? Not a problem if you really can afford it, but are you sure that you can? If you haven't got a long-term financial plan in place that supports your current spending level then the answer is that you don't.

Are you the miser? Do you not spend simply because you fear you can't afford it? Again, get yourself a proper financial plan in place and you will know where the right balance is between financial prudence and the reality that some fun things cost money.

Are you balanced and realistic? Then you understand the issues well enough to make pretty reasonable decisions. But again, you need a plan to back up your gut instincts and help you avoid making mistakes.

Most of us possess at least a couple of these personality traits – often changing depending upon the situation we find ourselves in e.g. some people let go at Christmas time, or whilst on holiday. But we need to understand why and when we might follow one behavioural type so we can adjust our actions accordingly.

COMMON PSYCHOLOGICAL/BEHAVIOURAL PITFALLS

There are many other, well-documented psychological biases which can adversely affect our financial decision-making – and which we are all occasionally subject to. If you know what they are, you are probably less likely to be adversely affected by them. Here's just a few:

- **Status Quo Bias**. This is the tendency to want to keep things the way they are.

- **Endowment Effect**. This is the tendency to consider something you own to be worth more than it would be if you didn't own it.

- **Regret Aversion**. This is the tendency to avoid taking an action due to a fear that in hindsight it will turn out to have been less than optimal.

- **Money Illusion**. This is confusion between "real" and actual changes in money. For example: you invested £1 and now x-years later it is worth £1.50. Now if that £1 had risen purely by the rate of inflation over that period then it would be worth £2 today. The fact that it is now only worth £1.50 means it is worth less in "real" terms – even though it has gone up in "actual" terms.

- **Confirmation Bias**. This is the tendency to look for, favour, and be overly persuaded by information that *confirms* your initial impressions. Conversely, we tend to ignore and dismiss information which tends to *disprove* our initial impressions.

- **Over-confidence**. This is the tendency to over-estimate our own abilities i.e. we aren't as smart as we think we are – especially prevalent in my experience when it comes to investing.

- **Optimism**. People tend to be overly optimistic about the future. This might also be termed "wishful thinking."

- **Information Cascades**. This is the tendency to ignore our own objective information and instead focus on emulating the actions of others. This is also known as "herding".

- **False Consensus**. This is the tendency to think that others are just like us.

- **Weakness of Will**. This is the tendency to consciously do things which we sincerely know are wrong. A non-financial example includes smoking cigarettes – we know we shouldn't do it but many do it anyway. A financial example includes living within our means – we know we should do it, but we often don't.

- **Credulity**. While we might like to believe that we are all perfectly rational, reality is far different. Unfortunately, we tend to be susceptible to the manipulative messages that the media and advertising industry put out.

THE CALL OF CONSUMERISM

If you encounter people who have, or appear to have, possessions, wealth or success – pay no attention – don't let it affect you. Decide what you want in life, make plans to achieve these goals and ignore what other people might be doing; especially those people who treat worldly goods as a measure of personal self-worth.

Quentin Crisp

"Never keep up with the Joneses. Drag them down to your level!"

But most of us like nice things – houses, cars, holidays, clothes etc. – and the media is full of people with no talent earning big bucks, so why can't we have these things too?

Advertising is a huge problem in today's materialistic society. We are constantly bombarded with adverts that effectively tell us that "to be better, happier, more successful, you need ..." They are all rubbish and we just need to realise that and concentrate on what truly makes us happy – regardless of what the rest of the world seems to be doing.

Edward Gibbon

"I am indeed rich, since my income is superior to my expense, and my expense is equal to my wishes."

There is nothing more liberating than sticking two fingers up at what the media would have us believe is the popular culture of today. This drive to be part of a conformist society is only a false ideology created by advertising anyway. What is important – the only thing that is important – is doing what makes you happy and fulfilled (assuming you can afford to do it of course.)

So, don't make yourself miserable, anxious and poor by following someone else's idea of what your life should look like – live your life on your terms.

BE HONEST ABOUT YOUR STRENGTHS AND WEAKNESSES

Whilst some people advocate a policy of improving weaknesses, no-one has the talent or the time to be good at everything so concentrate on doing what you do well – and outsource everything else. Delegation is, fortunately, one thing that most sports pros find natural – after all you do it at work on a daily basis.

If your weakness is that you just don't have the time, expertise and/or inclination to manage your own finances properly (and let's be honest, most people don't), then find yourself a good financial coach and delegate this job to them. Don't make the mistake of managing your money yourself if you really don't know what you are doing – or even worse, you think your financial skills are far greater than they actually are!

Creating and maintaining financial discipline is something a good financial adviser can help you with. They will help you analyse your current position, identify areas that need attention inc. bad habits, provide options so you can make informed decisions – and produce a plan for you to follow going forward. So if you are not comfortable, or not motivated to produce your own plan, engage the services of a professional to help you. I cover how to go about this in the next chapter – Training.

MONEY AND RELATIONSHIPS

My strong recommendation is never to mix money and friendship/family unless you really have to. It is easy to assume that we all feel the same way about money but that is simply not the case – and, as I have already explained, money is a very emotional subject. Even the simplest of misunderstandings can cause real problems and ruin relationships. If you have to mix the two, treat it like a business transaction and have clear guidelines and agreements in place so you both know what you expect from each other.

If you are in a relationship then money is something you will need to talk about – even though many people seem to find it easier to talk about just about anything other than their finances. Remember – disagreements over money cause a lot of relationship breakdowns.

It might seem unromantic but it is both realistic and very necessary to discuss money management openly and honestly. You need to ensure you are both on the same wavelength, or if you are not, that this fact is highlighted and agreement reached on how you are going to proceed. Ignoring this issue can lead to misunderstanding, resentment and frustration.

So before you get too emotionally committed, or before you make any big financial decisions together, talk about money. You might not agree on everything but you need to make sure you at least share the same significant, fundamental values.

HOW TO DEAL WITH IT ALL –
THE PSYCHOLOGY OF EARNING LOTS

But what if you are not struggling financially? What if you are in fact earning a good/very good income?

If you are lucky enough to be earning "good money" – perhaps more than your parents ever did, then it can feel like an intoxicating mix of fear and excitement. It can all be a bit overwhelming.

For the rare few, professional and financial success can come very quickly and at a relatively young age. Now, as a parent myself, I can't think of anything I want more than my two children being successful at a job that they love doing. But the last thing I want is for them to get lots of money before they are equipped to handle it (not unless they had a good financial planner on-board of course).

When it comes to money we can often be our own worst enemy. Sometimes we just can't help but be influenced by our emotions – many of which are subtle in their influence.

But effective money management requires emotional discipline. And there is no doubt that a large and relatively sudden increase in income or wealth is far more difficult, emotionally, to cope with than a gradual increase.

If you doubt me, just ask yourself why is it that so many lottery winners have blown their fortune? Were they all stupid – did they blast it all in a short-term orgy of financial recklessness?

Oscar Wilde

"Anyone who lives within their means suffers from a lack of imagination."

Well yes, some of them, but most simply didn't manage it and/or themselves properly.

Of course the initial rush of wealth is fantastic – perhaps more money than you ever dreamed of and an ability to buy such wonderful things – homes, cars, jewellery, holidays etc.

I am not saying you shouldn't enjoy these things – after all you may have worked hard for them – but you also need to be realistic about what your future life may be like and your ability to fund it from what might be far lower earnings.

If it is likely that you are going to earn significantly more during your sporting career than you will subsequently, it is vitally important that you save a significant proportion of your sporting earnings. It will be the funds saved during this time that will enable you to maintain your desired standard of lifestyle after retirement. It is also worth thinking about trying to pay for some of those big expenses, or at least a good chunk of them, whilst your earnings are high e.g. a house purchase.

Reality can kick in pretty quickly. At some point, hopefully not too late, you will start to realise that you don't want to give up your nice lifestyle – but that you could so easily be forced to do so if you don't manage your finances properly now.

People have often told me that they feel an overwhelming responsibility not to mess up – especially those with families to support. These are the people who I know will plan properly and realistically – I don't need to worry about them because they appreciate how important good financial management is.

It is the people who never question whether they can afford it; never look beyond today – blindly believing that they will always have lots of money. These are the people who are likely to end up with real problems some way down the line.

Edmund Stockdale

"Money isn't everything, but it's a long way ahead of what comes next."

You owe it to yourself, and your family (or future family), never to be in the position of looking back at your career wishing you had taken your financial management more seriously – because at that point it will probably be too late.

CONCLUSIONS

You should now have a good idea of where you currently stand financially, what shape you are in, and perhaps some areas where you can, or need to, make some improvements.

You know exactly what your money currently does for you – as well as perhaps a few ideas of what you would like it to do in the future.

Whilst these may be mainly materialistic benefits, writing them down, and seeing them in "black and white" should have helped – especially making the future goals clearer – more tangible.

Considering the implications of either achieving your goals, or not achieving them, should have helped you make an emotional connection to them – and this will now help motivate you.

And think about your own personality and the way you approach money management, as this should help you understand how you can cut out any bad habits and make following good financial practices much easier.

In the next chapter "Training" we look at how we can use the information and knowledge you have gained so far to build a Financial Plan that will help you make the most of your money and achieve your life goals.

EXERCISES – KEY IDEAS – ACTIVITIES

1. Review your Income and Expenditure – are you living within your means?

2. Think about your own attitude towards money and especially discretionary spending. Are you striking a reasonable and realistic balance between living for today and planning for tomorrow?

3. Think about what money provides you with at the moment and why those things are important to you.

4. Project yourself forward a few years and list what you need to achieve between now and then for you to be happy with your progress? Think about what it would be like if you don't achieve your goals – what would be the implications?

5. Consider your strengths and weaknesses and how you could organise your financial affairs to help you adopt better habits and make better choices in the future.

NOTES:

CHAPTER TWO

TRAINING

Acting with confidence is one of the greatest challenges we face because life provides us with a very few universal certainties and an almost infinite number and variety of uncertainties.

When dealing with money all we can do is make use of as much experience, expertise and resources as we can in order to address the fundamental question:

> *"Will the proposed strategy, action, product or investment increase or reduce our chances of achieving our goals?"*

WHY HAVE A "FINANCIAL PLAN"?

As with any investment made in life – your sporting career, a family, a home, an education – the best results are achieved by carefully constructing a plan and then following that plan consistently over time.

A well-crafted **Financial Plan** provides a broad context for making important financial decisions and achieving your long-term financial goals.

It will clearly describe the critical factors that shape and affect your financial choices.

It documents your goals, time-frames and tolerance for investment risk.

And it will set-out your investment philosophy and investment process – explaining what you are going to invest in and why.

Clearly articulating your goals and your plan to achieve them has a number of important benefits:

1. **It helps provide long-term discipline to your decision-making.** It ensures that rational analysis is the basis for your financial decisions, making you less likely to act on emotional responses to short-term or one-off events.

2. **It encourages effective communication.** Because it clarifies both the issues that are most important to you and the strategy that you will use to achieve them, it minimises any misunderstandings that may arise between you (by providing a reminder of what you are doing and why), you and your family, or you and your advisers.

3. **It allows you to accurately review your plan and gauge your progress.** Such evaluations may then indicate that changes are called for.

FINANCIAL "HEALTH CHECK"

A Financial Plan should consider all of the issues that could potentially have an impact on your fiscal health:

1. **Your aims and goals**
   Every aspect of your plan should be focussed on improving your chances of achieving these. It is important that they are qualified and quantified and "SMART."

2. **Your issues**
   Any specific issues that you wish to address as a matter of priority. It is not always possible, or practical, to try and tackle everything at once.

3. **Your family**
   Current issues or future goals and where these stand in your list of priorities e.g. school/uni fees, weddings, inheritances etc.

4. **Debt repayment**
   Creating a plan to repay any debts.

5. **Savings and investments**
   Establishing an investment philosophy and process – putting a savings plan in place.

6. **Retirement planning**
   Reviewing opportunities and threats to your retirement goals – this will be for post-sport as well as eventual retirement.

7. **Disaster planning**
   Considering potential threats to your financial well-being and ensuring your contingency plans are robust e.g. insurance protection.

8. **Taxation**
   Reviewing the opportunities and threats to your taxation goals.

9. **Estate planning**

   Considering what you would want to happen if you died. Ensuring your estate planning wishes are current and legally valid.

10. **Your support team**

    How to get good advice that can help you achieve your goals – whilst avoiding bad advice that can harm you.

HOW TO PUT TOGETHER YOUR FINANCIAL PLAN

As with any large task, getting started can be a bit daunting. Putting together a Financial Plan from scratch can seem like a herculean task but if you take it one step at a time you can break it down into manageable chunks.

Once you have put your plan together the first time, it is much simpler and easier to review and update it. I would suggest doing this at least once a year; but you should re-evaluate your plan, or at least the relevant sections of it, more frequently in the event that something significant happens e.g. pay rise, job change, move house, get married (divorced) etc.

PLAN ITEMS 1, 2 AND 3 – YOUR AIMS, GOALS, PRIORITY ISSUES AND FAMILY

We have already covered items 1-3 in the last chapter and you should therefore:

* Have a good understanding of where you stand right now – financially.
* You know how much income you have and how much you are spending and on what.
* You also know what your assets are and what money you owe and to whom.
* You have given some thought to what you might want to achieve in life (outside of sport) and to the likely/estimated cost of these aims and goals. You have also calculated what you need (or can) put aside out of your net income towards achieving these goals.

- And even if you don't know exactly what it is that you are saving for at this stage, you should at least appreciate the need to do so.

This information should be at the front of your mind as you start to put together your financial plan.

4 – DEBT REPAYMENT

If you have debt, and by that I primarily mean non-mortgage debt, then its repayment should be one of your main priorities.

To repay debt successfully you need a plan – what a surprise! But seriously, it is much easier to get a handle on it all and on the best way of repaying it, if you have sat down and thought about it a little first. Also, once you have a plan, even if it means you won't be debt free for some time, at least you know that you will be at some point – and this psychological "silver lining" is worth a lot.

Credit and store cards

Start by looking at those short-term, high-interest debts such as store cards and credit cards. I appreciate some people like to use cards but unless you pay off the debt every month you are likely to pay serious interest on the outstanding balance. And, whilst they might get you discounts on certain goods, the interest rates on store cards especially are scary!

Once again it is time for you to be honest with yourself and if you really don't need all of your cards, or you keep running up debts you can't repay in full each month, cut them up!

Other personal debt

If you have other forms of debt, for example a personal loan or car loan, then it is likely to be on a structured repayment basis. Find out what interest rate you are paying and what, if any, penalties there are for additional or early repayment.

Often companies will allow you to pay off a certain amount, over and above the normal figure, without penalising you. If you have spare money left over in your budget then consider increasing your payments to accelerate the loan repayment – even a small extra amount each month can dramatically reduce the time it takes to repay a debt (and the amount of interest you pay in the meantime).

Having a plan in place to tackle and repay your non-mortgage debt will help you become free sooner and save you a lot of interest in the process.

Accelerated repayment plan

You need to repay your debts which means putting something aside from your budget towards achieving this goal. Even if you are already doing this, are you paying enough and is it targeted at the right debt(s)?

Try identifying any additional cash that you could use for debt repayment. Have a look again at your discretionary expenditure – hopefully you will be able to see some ways that you could reduce or eliminate aspects of your current expenditure.

Whilst you might not be able to avoid fixed costs that does not mean that you cannot reduce them. Shopping around for food, utilities and insurance can reap significant savings – savings that you can also use to repay debt. And even if you have no debts, why on earth would you pay some big company more than you have to when you could be spending that money on yourself? So shop around anyway!

There are a multitude of on-line comparison sites that you can use to check the prices of just about anything. And it is always worth re-checking at least once a year. Don't think that just because you went with a competitive company last year that this year's renewal will also be good value – it is common practice for companies to have big sales drives and then hike their prices up once they have landed lots of new customers. They rely on people being too lazy and complacent to move again – don't fall for that trick.

Combining utilities and insurances can save you money e.g. house and contents, gas and electricity. Managing and paying your account on-line and/or via direct debit will also usually yield a discount.

Cutting down on your spending may not be pleasant but most people can make some changes without impacting too much on the overall quality of their lifestyle. You need to be disciplined and, if you apply some self-control and structure to your spending habits, you will probably find you really don't notice that much of a difference.

Any savings you make should immediately be put towards your debt repayment fund.

Need some help?

If you are struggling to put together a plan that will realistically allow you to repay your debts, or you just want to talk to someone about your situation, then you need to seek professional help.

There are many free debt counselling services that can help you whatever your situation. But make sure that you use one of the free services and never a commercial debt repayment company, as they will charge you a fee that will just make things worse. Start with The Citizens Advice Bureau and then, if serious, try the Debt Advice Foundation, National Debtline, My Money Steps, or Consumer Credit Counselling Services.

Mortgages

Unlike many other forms of debt, mortgages at least buy a tangible asset that have the ability to hold, or even increase in value over the longer-term. If debt could be good, then this is certainly the skinny latte of the financial liabilities that you could take on.

We consider buying property as an investment in the next chapter.

Getting good advice when buying a home is essential, especially if it is your first one. If you have a friend or family member who knows anything about property and/or property maintenance, then get them to look at it before you make an offer. So many people buy a home knowing that it "needs some work" but have no idea, or woefully under-estimate the cost of that work (and the vendor is unlikely to point out your mistake.) If you don't have anyone you can call on, and/or the property is older or more complicated, then get a building survey or structural survey. The better informed you are, the better decisions you will make.

Before you even go home shopping it can be a good idea to speak to a mortgage broker and get an idea of what money you could borrow and how much it will cost you to repay. You don't necessarily need to secure a mortgage offer in principal, although some people like to do this – and having the finance in place can help if you get into negotiations with the vendor.

There are two main types of mortgage – "repayment" or "interest only" mortgages; although it is rare that the latter would be suitable. But it is often when people start to get bombarded with terms like "fixed", "tracker", "capped", "discounted" and "offset" and are offered deals over varying time periods that they start to feel overwhelmed.

If you are unsure which mortgage option might be most suitable for you, seek independent, professional advice. Ideally seek the advice of several advisers and also talk to friends and family to get the benefit of their experience.

If you have a reasonable amount of cash on deposit, an "offset" mortgage, which effectively reduces the amount of mortgage debt you pay interest on by the balance of your savings account, can be an attractive option.

Some mortgages allow you to pay off a lump sum, whilst retaining the ability to draw down that money again if needs be. This can be useful if your income is sporadic e.g. bonuses, appearance fees etc.

Never just go along to your bank or building society and assume the deal they offer you is the most competitive. At the very least use one of the many on-line mortgage comparison systems to narrow down a likely list of the best deals and then call the top few to get more details and ensure you would actually qualify for these terms.

You could engage the services of an independent mortgage broker – do ensure they are truly independent though. Your association may well have negotiated a "deal" with a mortgage firm e.g. they won't charge a fee. But speaking to a few advisers will give you a good feel of what services are on offer and allow you to compare services and cost. You could then compare this professional advice against your own on-line findings to see whether it is indeed worth paying for.

A mortgage is probably the biggest debt you will ever take on and securing the best deal will yield significant monthly savings – similarly, getting it wrong can be costly. If you are even remotely unsure about what to do, seek professional, independent advice.

5 – YOUR SAVING AND INVESTMENT PLAN

Once you have implemented your debt repayment plan, you can start thinking about saving.

To be clear, you don't have to repay all your non-mortgage debt before you start saving – in fact having some money you can fall back on is essential. Often a compromise between debt repayment and savings can be the most sensible way forward.

Getting into the savings habit

Most of us are creatures of habit – once we get into the rhythm of doing something it usually becomes accepted practice pretty quickly. Changing existing habits, on the other hand, can be painful and uncomfortable.

You need to consider your existing savings habits. Are you really putting enough away, and putting it into the right places, to enable you to achieve your goals? If not, you are going to have to make changes and then stick with them until this new regime becomes habitual.

Having looked at your income and expenditure you need to allocate a proportion to savings. How much you should save will depend entirely on your personal situation but I suggest you aim for a minimum of 10% of net income.

Obviously you can only save if you have spare cash, but be honest with yourself – you can't have a lot of discretionary spending and still argue you have no spare money for saving. On the other hand, if you have significant excess income then you should be aiming to save a lot more than 10%. This is especially important if you are going to rely on money earned during your sporting career to help fund your post-sport life.

One of the easiest ways to get into the savings habit is to set up savings accounts and then direct debit mandates that will automatically transfer funds into these accounts, preferably on the same day that your income arrives. This way you do not miss having the income (as you effectively never had it), and very soon this "in-out" position becomes accepted reality. You probably won't even notice any big sacrifices or changes in your life and will get used to funding your life without this cash.

When your income increases above the historic norm e.g. a pay rise, bonus, sponsorship or endorsement payment etc. put a good percentage of this money away immediately. Again, you won't miss it if you move it straight away but you will find it much harder if you hold onto it for a while "just in case", and then try and save it.

Term is key

Once you have determined how much you can, and need, to save you can start to consider where to put that money.

The term, or expected duration of any savings, is very important when deciding where best to invest it. For funds that you might need access to in the short-term i.e. the next 2-3 years, there is realistically no other sensible choice than cash, or cash equivalent. However, if you can afford to put this money aside for longer than that, other potentially more lucrative investment assets are an option.

Your liquid safety net

No-one can predict the future, but bad stuff happens – often when you least expect it.

Whilst you obviously hope nothing too bad will happen, it would be foolhardy to ignore the possibility that you could get injured, lose your job, or lose some/all of your funding/sponsorship.

In these circumstances you need to have sufficient available cash to keep yourself afloat – at least for a short while whilst you sort things out. Think about it – you will already have enough on your plate and not being able to pay your bills will simply turn a stressful situation into a financial disaster.

I recommend keeping the equivalent of at least three months' worth of expenditure easily accessible in a cash account – preferably six months. Many people keep more – it all depends on what you can afford and what level makes you feel comfortable. But don't keep too much in cash over the long term as it is unlikely to maintain its real value against inflation.

Short-term capital expenditure

A cash account should also be the default choice for any funds that you might need access to within the next 2-3 years e.g. a car, house deposit, new sofa etc.

How to secure a good interest rate on your cash savings

If you are going to regularly keep a reasonable amount of your money in cash it is important that it attracts as good a rate of interest as possible. This is especially important during periods when the rate of inflation exceeds the net (i.e. after tax) return on cash, as your funds will effectively be going down in value every year.

There are a multitude of different accounts you can choose from but there are just three basic things you need to consider:

1. How long can I tie up my money for? Fixed term accounts e.g. 1-year, or those that require you to give a minimum amount of notice of withdrawal, often pay more interest but are no good if you need your cash in an

emergency. Possible option – split your funds between instant access and notice accounts.

2. What rate of interest will I get and is it a flat rate, or supplemented for a certain period? Some accounts will pay attractive rates of interest but only for a period, often 1-year – after which they often revert to a much lower rate. If this is the case then you need to make a diary note to move this money elsewhere at the end of the specified term.

3. Am I liable to pay tax on the interest? If you are a non-taxpayer then you can request that your interest be paid without the deduction of tax by completing a simple R85 form. If however, you do pay tax then you could consider putting some of your savings into a cash ISA (2014/15 personal limit is £5,940) as these accounts aren't liable to taxation.

One of the easiest ways to source and compare the available cash accounts is by using one of the multitudes of comparison websites. However, I would suggest comparing the results from at least two as, whilst the results should be the same, they often aren't.

Other investment options

By their very nature, some of your savings will be longer term and cash has historically been a poor long-term investment.

To get the best return on your money you will want to invest in other, potentially more rewarding assets. But you need to do this in a methodical and structured way if you are to secure these extra returns and not end up losing some/all of your money instead.

How to go about building an investment portfolio is a complex subject but one that you really should know a bit about, even if you intend to outsource this task to a professional. Ignorance is fine when things are going well but when markets crash and the value of your savings fall (which they most likely will at some point), how will you know whether your savings are safe, or whether they've been invested properly? The usual reaction is panic and this kind of emotional response often results in people making bad and costly decisions.

Not only will some basic knowledge help you understand the key issues, but it will undoubtedly help prepare you for what will be anything but a smooth ride.

There are a lot of myths and bad habits which can seriously damage your wealth – and you need to be aware of these. Many are perpetuated by elements of the banking and financial services industries – either because they don't know any better themselves; or because having such discussions with clients can be tricky and time consuming – and as they are getting paid regardless, why bother?

As I said at the start of this book, you don't need to be a financial expert but arming yourself with some basic knowledge will dramatically improve your chances of doing the right things and avoiding costly mistakes.

I strongly recommend that you read the next chapter "How to Successfully Invest Your Long-Term Savings."

Investment Products and Tax Wrappers

I have provided some basic information on "Financial Products" and "Tax Wrappers" in the "How to Successfully Invest Your Long-Term Savings" chapter of this book.

Choosing a product or tax wrapper should be the last decision that you make i.e. after you have decided what assets you are going to invest in. The only reason to use one is if it will benefit you in some way e.g. save you tax.

Before you think about products and tax wrappers you need to get your investment philosophy and process right. Once you know what you want to invest in, and why, then you will be in position to decide whether or not putting those investment assets in a tax wrapper or product would actually benefit you.

6 – RETIREMENT PLANNING

Retirement is a fundamentally different phase in our lives. The theory obviously being that after decades of hard work we are able to relax and "enjoy life." I think it works out for some but not so well for others, and usually the difference is "money."

But retirement planning is about more than just putting in place some form of savings schemes so that you can still pay your bills when you finally give up work. Money can fund a lifestyle but happiness in retirement often comes down to finding something(s) enjoyable and fulfilling to replace work.

When many people think about retirement planning they think "pensions" – and that can be a large part of it. But there are lots of ways you could fund your lifestyle when you retire and often people's income comes from several sources e.g. state pension, private pension, employer pension, savings/investments, rental income etc.

How important pensions are in someone's overall retirement plans will vary from person to person depending on their individual circumstances. For some people pensions provide the vast majority, if not all, of their retirement income. For some, pensions only play a minor role as the majority of their income comes from others sources e.g. savings, property, an inheritance, a business sale etc.

Pension schemes

In this chapter I am going to concentrate on pensions as this is the only arrangement specifically designed for retirement provision.

Pension funds have traditionally been used to save for one's eventual retirement. The reason people predominantly use pensions rather than other vehicles is because they come with tax benefits, and whilst many such benefits have been withdrawn or reduced over the years, the main one still remains (with a few caveats) – tax relief on your contributions.

With the exception of a few higher-risk, specialist types of investment (e.g. VCT and EIS schemes), no other form of saving plan benefits from tax relief on the money you pay in. So it is likely that putting some of your long-term savings into a pension is going to be a good idea.

Pension contributions are assumed to be paid out of basic rate taxed income i.e. when you pay £80 into a pension, the pensions company automatically claims the 20% tax back, so £100 is credited to your account. The same £100 only costs higher 40% rate taxpayers £60 (though you usually have to claim some of this back yourself).

The maximum you can contribute to a pension plan each year[1] and on which you can receive tax relief is 100% of your earnings (subject to a current cap of £40,000 in the 2014/15 tax year) or £3,600, whichever is greater. This means that even non-taxpayers can contribute up to £3,600 pa and get tax relief.

Basic rate and non-taxpayers get an instant 25% investment boost (i.e. pay £80, get £100) and higher rate taxpayers 67%. This is why pensions should be taken seriously.

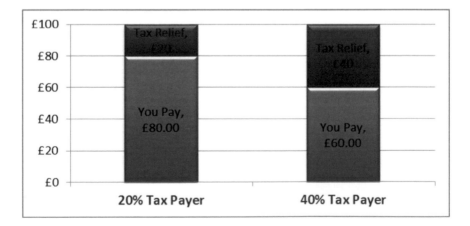

[1]   *The annual pension contribution allowance test isn't based on payments made in the tax year – it's what's paid in the pension input period (PIP) ending in the tax year that matters.*

Salary sacrifice – the extra boost

Sometimes it is possible, with the agreement and co-operation of your employer, to give up some of your earnings in return for pension contributions – out of your PRE-TAX salary. This can be attractive for both parties because, not only do you avoid tax on your contribution, but neither you nor your employer pays National Insurance (NI) on this amount either.

- **Basic rate taxpayers:** This means that for every £680 of pay you sacrifice, £1,000 goes into your pension pot.

- **Higher rate taxpayers:** If you pay tax at the higher 40% rate, salary sacrifice means you don't have to claim back the extra tax relief yourself – it happens automatically. To deposit £1,000 in your pension pot, you only have to give up £580 from your pay packet.

Above calculations based on 2014/15 income tax and National Insurance rates and assumes any salary sacrifice would have been fully liable to both taxes.

However, one thing to consider is that by taking salary sacrifice you would be taking an effective pay cut – albeit to get a great benefit back. But having a lower headline salary can potentially cause problems – for example, if you are about to receive maternity pay, or apply for a mortgage, then you should think twice before sacrificing.

Group and employer pension schemes

You may have access to a pension through your club or association. Often these are good schemes, with the most attractive being those that provide additional contributions from your employer – usually on the basis that if you pay in X, then they will pay Y. For example, under the England and Wales Cricket Board Group Personal Pension, county clubs will contribute 10% of a player's annual earnings if they contribute a minimum of 5% – which compared to most private sector schemes is incredibly attractive.

If you are employed and your club doesn't currently offer a pension then this will change over the next few years as the government gradually introduces Pension Auto-Enrolment – a scheme that will compel employers to setup and automatically enrol employees into a pension arrangement. Importantly the rules insist that there are minimum contributions made by both employee and employer.

But if you don't have access to a group/employer pension, or perhaps you want to top up your contributions using an alternative arrangement, then you will need a private pension.

The different types of private pension

There are two main types of private pension – many auto-enrolment schemes are likely to be a group variation of the first:

- **Personal Pensions and Stakeholders.**
  Pension providers set plans up and offer you a choice of funds to invest in – this can be anything from just their own in-house fund range to a carte-blanche choice of providers, funds and even individual shares. The main difference between personal and stakeholder pensions is that with stakeholder the provider's annual charge is capped at 1.5% of the pension's value and they must allow easy transfers of investments between funds and providers. Stakeholder plans also usually have a default investment fund – which is where the provider will invest your contributions if you don't choose your own fund(s). But apart from this there is often little difference between many schemes, so it is better to ignore what it is called and concentrate on the level of charges and ensuring that you have access to a suitable range of investment funds.

- **SIPPs provide greater flexibility**
  Self-Invested Personal Pensions (SIPPs) allow you to invest in a wide range of investments from a government approved list – which includes any UK approved investment fund, individual shares and even land and commercial property. These schemes are primarily for those with larger

pension pots and can be especially useful for those who can use their pension funds to help with their business planning e.g. buy their business premises. But with the increased options and investment flexibility comes greater regulation and monitoring, which in turn often leads to higher charges. So, if you are never really going to use, or benefit from the "self-investment" option you are probably better off choosing a personal or stakeholder pension.

How should I invest my pension monies?

Being a long-term investment you will want to invest the majority of your pension monies in other, potentially more rewarding assets than cash. But you need to invest wisely and logically if you are to maximise returns and minimise risk. Even a small difference in annual return, multiplied over decades of investment, can hugely alter the final value of your retirement fund.

Read Chapter 2a – How to Successfully Invest Your Long-Term Savings.

Is there a maximum I can put into pensions?

There is a limit on the value you can accrue in approved pension schemes before tax penalties apply. That limit is called the Lifetime Allowance.

The Lifetime Allowance is reduced to £1.25m from 6th April 2014. The table on page 64 shows the Lifetime Allowance for past tax years.

At the time of payment, a recovery charge will be applied to the value of your retirement funds in excess of the Lifetime Allowance. The amount will depend on how the excess is paid.

If it is paid in the form of a pension, the excess will be subject to a 25% tax charge and the income will also be subject to Income Tax. For example, if you had a pension fund of £1.65 million in 2015, £400,000 would be subject to the tax charge of 25% (tax due £100,000), leaving £1.55 million to provide a taxable income.

TAX YEAR	LIFETIME ALLOWANCE
2006/2007	£1.50m
2007/2008	£1.60m
2008/2009	£1.65m
2009/2010	£1.75m
2010/11 and 2011/12	£1.80m
2012/2013	£1.50m
2014/2015	£1.25m

If the excess is paid as a lump sum, it will be subject to a one-off 55% recovery charge. For example, if you had a pension fund of £1.65 million in 2015, £400,000 would be subject to the tax charge of 55% (tax due £220,000), leaving a lump sum of £180,000.

With such punitive charges, it is essential you consider whether the total value of your pension funds may breach the Lifetime Allowance limit sometime in the future.

When can I take my pension benefits?

From April 2010 the minimum age that retirement benefits can be taken from a pension scheme/plan is now 55; or earlier due to ill health.

Traditionally, professional sportspeople were allowed to take benefits earlier than this. There are still transitional arrangements for those with schemes that were setup with earlier retirement dates (i.e. those before 6th April 2006 – A Day), but there are strict rules on what you can do to these without re-setting the retirement date to age 55 – so always check with your provider or adviser before making any changes to these plans. The "lifetime allowance", which is the total amount of money you can save in a pension without being penalised, will also be reduced by 2.5% for each year benefits are taken before age 55.

Not being able to draw benefits from your pension plan when you retire from sport makes planning ahead essential. Proper preparation will help you secure a follow-on career that is both personally and financially rewarding. Getting your non-pension finances in good order will ensure you'll be able to fund your desired lifestyle – even if your initial post-sport career income is lower.

7 – DISASTER PLANNING

Life isn't always fair and bad stuff can and does happen. All any of us can do is consider the risks that we face and ensure that we are properly prepared for them.

If you have followed the advice given earlier in this book then you will have, or be working towards having, three to six months' savings in an accessible cash account. This invaluable resource can take a lot of the initial pressure off, allow you time to come to terms with whatever has happened, and work towards a solution.

Hopefully, whatever pitfalls you face will be small and/or short-lived, but sometimes this is not the case.

There are three main disasters that you need to plan for:

1.   You are able to compete but you lose all/part of your income.

2.   Inability to compete due to illness or injury.

3.   Death.

LOSING YOUR JOB AND/OR YOUR FUNDING

There can be many reasons why your job or your funding might not exist tomorrow and some of them are completely outside of your control. What would you do if you were told today that your contract wasn't going to be renewed, or that your funding was being cut or withdrawn in the near future? How would you fund your on-going expenditure?

You need to ask yourself these types of questions and formulate some sort of plan as to how you would react. It may not be a total solution, but at least thinking this scenario through will mean you are better prepared to cope and deal with this problem when (as you will retire either voluntarily or involuntarily at some point), it happens to you.

Think about practical things you could do – and how you could improve on them. Where could you potentially find alternative employment and/or funding? What marketable skills, qualifications and/or achievements have you got? How much could you cut from your budget in order to economise? What benefits could you be entitled to and what do you need to do in order to qualify? E.g. pay National Insurance contributions.

You might find that this process also gives you some positive ideas for things you could do now. Perhaps something you would like to do as a hobby or an alternative career; some simple and painless ways to save money; or other potential sources of income. We consider work and post-sport planning in the Performance chapter.

INJURY OR ILLNESS

Injuries are inevitable – constantly pushing your body will inexorably mean pushing it past its limit at some point. The only uncertainties are: how often, how bad and how long will it take to recover?

If you do get injured, there are three things you need to address:

1. Treatment – getting the injury assessed and a course of treatment and rehabilitation organised.

2. Emotional support – being side-lined can be stressful and the longer it goes on the harder it can be to deal with.

3. Financial support – making sure that you can continue to pay your bills whilst you recover.

Getting treatment

If you are ill or injured then obviously your first priority is to get appropriate medical treatment. One of the perks of being a pro sports person is that you probably have access to some of the best medical resources available. Injuries are assessed and diagnosed very quickly and the appropriate treatment and rehabilitation delivered by top specialists. This has dramatically reduced the number of chronic long-term injuries, but obviously nothing will ever prevent them.

Emotional support

Not being able to do what you love to do is frustrating. And injuries don't come with a guarantee that says "do this and in X time you will be alright" – they are unpredictable in recovery.

This uncertainty – not knowing how long it will take – whether you will be fully fit in time for the big match – will you still have your place in the team when you get back – will you carry an inherent weakness in that area from now on – all of this is hugely stressful.

But the tendency can be to keep these worries to yourself. For whatever reason – pride, embarrassment, mis-placed bravado, being British – some people just don't feel comfortable talking about how they feel. And of course the prospect of baring your emotional soul can be a bit daunting, you are purposefully making yourself vulnerable, but we all need to do it at some point during our lives. You have access to excellent support in your fellow pros, clubs and associations and this can make a huge difference in these circumstances. These people know, often through personal experience, what you are going through – what it is like to be an injured sports pro.

Just talking about how you are feeling can be hugely cathartic. So, if you do find yourself worried about injury, find someone you are comfortable talking to and tell them how you are feeling. If you don't know anyone, contact your club or association and they will be able to recommend someone. I guarantee that they will do everything they can to help and support you.

Financial support

When you're playing a highly physical, high intensity sport the chances of injury and an extended period away from sport are considerable. That means it's important to consider how you are going to pay the bills when you can't compete.

In most cases you are likely to continue to receive at least a proportion of your wages/funding for a limited period – but you need to check with your club/association/funding organisation to ascertain the exact terms. The problems start when your injury or illness keeps you out for longer and this income dries up. How are you going to continue paying your bills?

You need to calculate how much money you would need in order to continue paying the bills and when you would need this alternative source of income to start e.g. after 26 weeks. Perhaps you would have access to some measure of financial support should you be unable to compete long term e.g. savings, family etc. And whilst an injury might put a hold/end to your sporting career, you would probably still be able to take on some form of employment.

If after assessing the potential risk that long-term injury poses to you, you find that you would be unable to fund your lifestyle, then you should seriously consider insuring yourself against this possibility.

DEATH

I appreciate when you are young you feel invincible and even contemplating death must seem ridiculous. But the fact is that most people know of at least one person who has died either suddenly, or at a young age – I lost four school friends under the age of forty.

It might not be a nice thing to think about but planning for this eventuality is important. You need to consider both the financial and personal ramifications of your death.

- Would the result be disaster?

- Could your family cope, but only by struggling by?

- Perhaps, at this stage in your life, there would be no financial blow-back on anyone else.

I cover Estate Planning (the planning and paperwork aspects of death) in more detail later in this chapter – here I want you to purely think about the financial consequences.

Many clubs or associations provide some form of life assurance – often alongside a pension scheme. This would provide a lump sum in the event of your death, which can be used to pay off debts and help fund on-going lifestyle costs for those left behind.

You need to find out what insurance you are entitled to and then compare this with your own situation. Work out what debts would need/want to be fully/partially repaid. And whether those you would leave behind would need some extra cash – at least for a while – to help them meet their monthly bills. The total "liability gap" gives you an idea of the level of insurance cover that you need to have in place.

And make sure you keep nominations and trusts on all pension and insurance schemes up-to-date. These are your instructions as to where the benefits should go and, whilst easily over-looked, having these schemes is of little benefit if the proceeds get paid to the wrong person.

INSURANCE

Not the most enthralling subject but life carries risk and you just can't ignore the financial consequences of death, serious illness or serious/long-term injury.

But insurance costs money and sometimes a lot of money. So what risks should you insure against and how much protection should you get?

My personal view is that *"insurance is there to protect you and your family against unacceptable risk"* – whether that be the risk itself, or the size of that risk.

You need to start by assessing what risks you face and the financial impact they could have on your life. This is where your income, expenditure and balance sheet work comes into their own – you should now know what your outgoings are and also what debts/liabilities you have.

Once you know what the potential risks are and also their size, you can decide whether to insure against all of those risks or perhaps just insure a portion and accept the rest yourself.

For example, you might decide that you want to take out life assurance to cover the whole of your mortgage debt in the event of your serious illness and/or death. On the other hand, because the cost of injury insurance is so high you might decide to take out insurance to cover just 50% of your total income needs – accepting that you will somehow have to find the rest yourself should something happen.

Most clubs and/or associations have links with specialist insurance brokers or companies that can provide cover designed especially for pro sportspeople.

Insurance schemes to meet every need

Insurance is something you need to take professional advice about. An experienced adviser will help you assess your needs and recommend suitable solutions. He/she should (if independent) also make sure that you get the best cover for the most competitive price. But, as I keep suggesting all through this book, if you have thought about this issue a bit yourself you will be better able to assess the quality of their advice and, as a result, be happier that you have been properly taken care of.

There are lots of different types and variations of insurance contract – enabling you to tailor cover to your specific needs. Because there are so many varieties the following is not meant to be a definitive list but simply a basic explanation of some of the more common insurances people use.

Life Assurance

A contract that pays a specified sum upon your death – often used for family protection, to cover debts or provide compensation.

There are many different types of life assurance contract – some simply pay a one-off lump sum, whilst others will make an annual payment for a specified time (Family Income Cover.) The level of cover can be fixed, increasing e.g. by inflation, or decreasing – the latter often used to cover a reducing mortgage debt.

Some contracts even include an element of savings – although I have never seen the appeal/sense in mixing protection and investing.

Critical/Serious Illness

Similar schemes to life assurance and used for the same reasons – but these pay out in the event that you suffer from one of a specified list of illnesses/conditions e.g. cancer, heart-disease, stroke etc.

The possibility of surviving a critical illness before age 65 is almost twice as great as dying. A serious illness can have a devastating effect on your life – often requiring lengthy treatment and recuperation during which time you may not be able, or fit to do too much else. Sometimes no cure is possible. These contracts provide cash at a time when it is often needed the most.

People will often choose to have both life assurance and critical illness cover to provide broad protection.

Income Protection

Whilst many clubs and/or associations will continue paying income for a limited period, they will not do so indefinitely. This policy will provide a replacement income to cover your monthly regular outgoings should you find yourself suddenly unable to work due to accident, sickness, injury or even unemployment.

Some sports provide limited income protection insurance cover, but recommend pros take out additional cover themselves. Many sports don't provide insurance cover at all – leaving this decision up to the individual.

Gordon Taylor OBE, PFA Chief Executive

"Every player runs the risk of career-ending injury….. We believe all players should have their own …. policy ….to insure against the loss of future career earnings and secure their future. This type of cover is particularly important for young players…"

You should know what benefits your club or association provides – you can then decide whether they are sufficient for your needs.

Private Medical Insurance

Whilst you will have access to excellent medical care, this may not extend to non-sporting problems. Obviously we have a pretty good health service in the UK but some people prefer the choice, speed and peace of mind offered by private facilities.

There are various types of private health insurance contract that can help pay for, or at least protect you against more costly procedures and treatment. They offer a wide range of cover and benefits, so if you are potentially interested in this type of insurance I suggest finding a local specialist to help and advise you.

CLUB AND ASSOCIATION BENEFITS

Most clubs and associations provide excellent support and a wealth of useful resources. I don't think many pros realise just how lucky they are – outside your world this level of help is rare indeed.

Whilst they do make great efforts to communicate what is on offer to their members, you also have a responsibility to make yourself fully aware of what is available – and to take advantage.

"Help and resources are all around us. You just need to ask for the help and then use the resources."

Club and association pension and insurance schemes provide an excellent starting point. Some offer very generous arrangements – others less so. You need to check what yours provides for you.

The temptation can be to assume whatever your club/association provides in the way of pension or insurance is sufficient and that you don't need to do any further financial planning. But often these schemes are only there to provide a basic foundation – it is important that you compare your individual needs and identify any shortcomings in provision.

Here are just a few of the areas of support available:

- Legal advice – contracts, criminal, media, wills.
- Agent advice – from choosing one, to contract advice, to disputes.
- Insurance advice – often provided by specialist advisers.
- Pension, Life Assurance and Income Protection insurance – many operate schemes for their members.
- Banking – often free/subsidised banking.
- Tax advice – tax returns and general tax advice.
- Financial advice – from mortgages, to general financial advice and investment management.
- Medical advice – advice, treatment and help with long term injuries.
- Overseas – advice on working and living abroad.
- Drug and illicit substance advice – personal and general anti-doping policy.
- Psychological health – confidential and professional help and advice.
- Player development – sporting and post-sport career advice and practical support – often confidential helpline.
- Business advice – thinking of starting your own business, or investing in someone else's?
- Job opportunities – advertising and support.
- Media – help and advice about dealing with the press.
- Member newsletters and magazines.

Some of the services and benefits are provided by the clubs/associations themselves and some by "corporate" or "preferred" partners. If it is the latter, ask what the connection and advantage is of using these firms – often they are specialists, or offer free/subsidised services.

Why not give your local contact a call today and have a chat about what they can help you with?

BENEVOLENT FUNDS

Many sports have established benevolent funds to help current and former players and their dependants in times of hardship, upheaval or to re-adjust to the world beyond the game.

Benevolent issues pull at everyone's heart strings and the various associations, clubs and members do an awful lot to generate funds for these important charities.

They can provide financial help and practical support to present and former pros in the following areas:

- Emergency relief for sudden catastrophic or life-changing injury.

- Help with the cost of on-going medical treatment as a result of long-term illness or injury.

- Financial hardship if unable to work as a result of illness or injury.

- A free and confidential counselling service.

- Support to attain educational qualifications and training.

Hopefully your involvement with your sports benevolent fund will solely be in the role of support and fund raising – but do get involved. You never know when you, or a colleague, might need help.

8 – TAX PLANNING

Are you employed or self-employed? And what sources of income do you have?

If you are employed and don't have any source of income other than that paid to you via your club, then your affairs are likely to be pretty straight forward. Tax and National Insurance will be deducted from your wages via the PAYE (pay as you earn) system – you probably don't need to do anything else. But if you are self-employed, have additional sources of income, or have income above a certain level, then you may need to complete a tax return.

If you have got an accountant or book keeper then you should be getting individual advice about what paperwork you need to submit to the HMRC and also on how best to arrange your tax affairs. Often this is pretty straight forward –

what needs declaring; what expenses you can claim; how to arrange income and savings to make them tax efficient e.g. set up a limited company, transfer taxable savings into a tax wrapper like an ISA etc.

If you don't have an adviser and want some advice, one of the best places to start is the HMRC self-assessment website –www.hmrc.gov.uk/sa/introduction.htm Or you can call the HMRC Self-Assessment helpline: 0845 900 0444.

National Insurance contributions

National Insurance is a scheme where people in work make payments towards benefits. The payments are called National Insurance contributions and certain state benefits are only payable if you meet the National Insurance contribution conditions. So it is important that you pay the right amount, or get credits if you are not liable to pay contributions.

If you are employed then the correct type and level of National Insurance contributions will be automatically deducted from your wages via PAYE. If you are self-employed, or have some self-employed earnings, then you may be liable, or it may be advisable, for you to pay self-employed National Insurance on this income.

Even if you are not liable to pay National Insurance, gaps in your National Insurance record can prevent you from getting benefits and affect your State Pension. If you are in this situation then you should contact the HMRC and see if you are eligible to claim credits to fill any gaps in your contribution record.

HMRC has a number of telephone helplines where you can get advice and information about National Insurance. You can find more information about National Insurance contributions and get details of the helplines on the HMRC website at: www.hmrc.gov.uk

Tax Mitigation

It can be easy to confuse sensible tax management, or tax avoidance, with tax evasion – the first two being perfectly acceptable and legal, whilst the latter being illegal and immoral. You have a legal right to pay no more tax than is necessary – you just don't have a right to evade it altogether.

Lord Clyde ruling in case Ayrshire Pullman Motor Services and Ritchie v. IRC

"No man in this country is under the smallest obligation, moral or other, so to arrange his legal relations to his business or to his property as to enable the Inland Revenue to put the largest possible shovel into his stores."

The problem can be telling the difference between acceptable (morally and legally) and unacceptable. The issues are often so complex that lay people have no chance of telling the difference, so they rely completely on their advisers. Unfortunately, these advisers, in turn, sometimes rely on the advice of their specialist adviser. And occasionally they do not properly explain (or understand) the risks involved with tax avoidance schemes that often rely on questionable loopholes.

Personally, I like to categorise tax schemes – it makes them easier to understand:

Green – perfectly reasonable and acceptable practices; often actively encouraged by the government e.g. using up your personal allowances, claiming legitimate expenses and investing in tax efficient schemes like pensions and ISAs.

Amber – schemes that do not break any laws but rather exploit loopholes and badly worded legislation. Whilst you would be doing nothing wrong by using these schemes you would be flouting the spirit of the law and therefore run the risk that the HMRC will challenge you.

Red – whilst these schemes may not be illegal the methods they use are so blatantly contrary to tax law and common sense that you are just asking to be challenged. In my view, many of these arrangements are as good as tax evasion.

Most people, I think, are happy to pay a reasonable amount of tax – they just don't want to pay any more than they have to. And there is a lot you can do to ensure your affairs are run efficiently so as to achieve this goal – something a good tax/financial adviser will be able to help you with.

For those who try and push the boundaries of acceptability there is always the risk of HMRC challenge – which can potentially lead to a lengthy and costly battle and, if the HMRC wins, reclaim of tax due plus interest and fines. A lot of the time you won't even know whether you have "got away with it" for years afterwards – you can be in 6-8 years of costly "discussions" with the HMRC.

The government and HMRC are determined to change the culture of tax evasion/avoidance and have already clamped down hard on many schemes. New "Anti Abuse" legislation and additional investment will enable HMRC to tackle people who invest in schemes that might follow the letter of the law, but not the spirit of the law.

Basic tax management is a right and should be an important part of your Financial Plan. But be very careful when considering any method of tax minimisation/avoidance that doesn't come with a clear stamp of government approval.

Finally, if you have a large, untaxed windfall e.g. sponsorship lump sum, or bonus, find out how much tax you are likely to owe on that money and put that much in a cash deposit account. Don't spend it all now then find you don't have the money to pay the tax when the demand comes in.

9 – ESTATE AND INHERITANCE TAX PLANNING

I appreciate you might be wondering why I bothered to include a section on estate planning. Well, mainly because you should probably have a will, and even if much of the rest of this chapter doesn't currently apply to you, it will at some point – and in the meantime it might be useful for your parents/grandparents.

Wills – the bare minimum

If you have a spouse or partner, children, a home or business, or any people or causes that you want to care for after death, you need a will. Don't put it off. Make a will now so that your loved ones will remember you fondly rather than regretting your lack of foresight.

Many people mistakenly think that they don't need a will – that their affairs would be distributed "reasonably" for the benefit of their loved ones if they died. But if you die without one, your assets will be distributed according to the law rather than your wishes.

By having a will, you can control what happens to your property and possessions after you die, and it is the only way to make sure your family and friends are provided for in the way that you want following your death.

If you die without a will you're said to have died 'intestate' and the rules of intestacy will apply. If this happens, the law sets out who should deal with the deceased's affairs and who should inherit their estate. In addition, the intestacy provisions are complex and can make the administration of a person's estate more expensive. For example, under intestacy, marriage does not necessarily mean that all of your assets and possessions will pass to your spouse – a common misconception.

There are three ways to make a will. You can buy a DIY form from a stationery shop, consult with a company that specialises in wills, or hire a solicitor. I recommend the third option.

A solicitor may be able to give you additional advice and they will ensure that your will is legally binding – which it might not be if you go down the DIY route. And using a solicitor need not be prohibitively expensive if you plan thoughtfully in advance.

Many clubs/associations have links with lawyers who offer members free/discounted will services. This offer can give you the peace of mind that your will is drafted accurately and specifically to your requirements.

Wills FAQ's

What is a will?
A will is a legal document that comes into effect on your death. By making a will you are deciding who should look after your affairs after you've died (your Executors).

Who should have a will?

Everyone over the age of 18 should make a will. Even if you have made a will, you should review it regularly to make sure that it reflects your current circumstances and wishes.

Why is it important?

To ensure that your assets and property pass to the people you choose.
If you're unmarried you can make sure your partner is provided for. Without a will unmarried partners would not inherit any of your estate.
To make provision for the guardianship of children in the event that both parents are killed. To plan effectively for a possible Inheritance Tax liability.

Keeping your will up to date

Having made a will it is very important that you review it regularly. Major life events can have a significant impact on your existing will, and you should consider making or amending it in the event of:

- Marriage – if you have married or entered into a civil partnership since your will was prepared, your will is automatically revoked unless it specifically states that it has been made in contemplation of marriage.

- Cohabitation – unmarried partners or civil partners do not benefit under the rules of intestacy. Therefore, if you cohabit with someone and you want them to benefit from your estate after your death, you should make a will.

- Divorce – unlike marriage, divorce does not revoke a will until a 'decree absolute' has been made or a 'decree of dissolution' in the case of civil partnerships.

- Becoming a parent – if you're a parent, or are to become one, you should amend your will to make sure your child or children will be looked after following your death. It is common for wills to make provisions for any of the deceased's surviving children or grandchildren. However, if you have specifically named children or grandchildren, any further children or grandchildren that may have been born will not benefit from your estate, unless a new will or codicil (a legal addition to an existing will), is prepared.

A basic estate planning checklist:

1. Make a will.
The process of putting a will in place necessitates the gathering of information, its analysis and then the consideration of many important aspects of your personal and financial life. Simply by doing this you will address a lot of practical issues and maybe highlight some areas that still need additional planning e.g. minimising your inheritance tax liability.

2. Consider a trust.
Trusts can have all kinds of potential advantages – from saving tax to ensuring your assets go to the people you want them to; and/or are used in the way you want them to be used. However, the use of, and suitability, of trusts requires expert advice.

3. Make health care directives.
Setting out your wishes should you become unable to make medical decisions for yourself. Health care directives include a health care declaration ("living will") and a power of attorney for health care, which gives someone you choose the power to make decisions if you can't.

4. Make a power of attorney.
You can give a trusted person authority to handle your finances and property if you become incapacitated and unable to manage your own affairs.

5. Protect your children's property.
You should name an adult to manage any money and property your minor i.e. under age 18, children may inherit from you.

6. File beneficiary or trust forms.
Naming a beneficiary, or writing an insurance or pension policy under trust, will enable "death benefits" to be paid directly to your beneficiary and allows the funds to skip the probate process – this saves time and avoids inheritance tax.

7. Make final arrangements.
Make your wishes known regarding organ and body donation and disposition of your body – burial or cremation. This can be included in your will.

8. Store your documents carefully.
Your partner, solicitor and/or your executor (the person you choose in your will to administer your property after you die) will need access to documents such as:

- Will.
- Birth and marriage certificates.
- Passports.
- Trusts/nominations.
- Insurance policies.
- Property deeds.
- Certificates and latest statements for investments.
- Information on bank accounts, savings accounts and safe deposit boxes.
- Information on retirement plans.
- Information on debts: credit cards, mortgages and loans, utilities, and unpaid taxes.
- Information and latest statements for all utility providers.
- Information on any final arrangements you have made, or burial wishes.

9. Disaster folder.
One of the most difficult, time consuming and costly roles for family members and executors is gathering the information required to settle an estate. In addition to all of the above documents, prepare a list of all passwords, PIN numbers and any other confidential bits of information that your wife, partner, executor or solicitor might need to access or manage your financial affairs. *Obviously make sure that you keep this sort of sensitive information secure – very secure!*

Further planning and inheritance tax mitigation

Further estate and inheritance tax planning is a specialist area and one which you need to take expert advice. Often the issues span both the legal and financial arenas – so you need to ensure that you either engage someone who has expertise in both; or get your financial adviser and solicitor to work together.

10 – CHOOSING YOUR SUPPORT TEAM

Warren Buffett, Business Magnate, Investor and Philanthropist

"Good advice is a great investment."

When should you seek advice? How do you know who to trust? These are very hard questions to answer – but incredibly important ones for you to figure out.

Professional sportspeople generally recognise the value of good advice and of the benefits of delegation. You appreciate that other people are better than you at some things and willingly defer to their experience and expertise.

Adam Shore, Former in-House Legal Council to BAR Honda Formula 1

"Choose your advisers very carefully – it can be disruptive and expensive if you get it wrong."

This propensity can however be a bad trait as well as a good one. Unfortunately not everybody is as good as they say they are (or you think/hope they are), and you can therefore end up relying on a service or advice that is not as good as it should be. Also, not everybody will have your best interests in mind – their actions/guidance can sometimes be tainted with self-interest.

You need to go through a due diligence process before acting on any advice you receive, or handing over responsibility for part of your life to someone. After all, if things go wrong it will be you who will pay the price – whether that just means increased hassle, or missed opportunities, or financial loss.

Whilst it may well be an area in which you have little knowledge, or are not comfortable with (hence the decision to seek advice or delegate), just asking a few simple, logical questions can make all the difference. It will help filter the good from the not so good and ensure you get the best advice and support instead of a bad and potentially costly experience.

The golden rules

"Never just accept advice at face value."

Ask questions to help you determine whether that advice might really help YOU achieve YOUR goals.

If you are still unsure keep asking questions until you are.

And if you are still uncertain get a second opinion.

Why?

- Because we are all different and just because something worked (or didn't work) for that particular person doesn't mean the same will necessarily apply to you.
- People can contaminate (not always unintentionally), the advice they received from another source with their own prejudices or views; so what you get is a biased and potentially misleading version.
- Misinformation and plain bravado – it is surprising just how much c**p some people are happy to pass off as fact – especially when talking about subjects such as investing.

So how do you tell what is good advice and what is bad? Well, that is not always easy, but I think you can apply a simple rule that will help determine what information to take on-board and what you need to be wary of.

If the subject is one in which this person has personal experience, or expertise, then it is probably worth listening to what they have to say (note – I didn't say "do what they advise"), e.g. an experienced player, or association rep giving you advice on how to choose an agent.

If, however, this is an area that they are not experienced or an expert in e.g. investing, then be wary and never act until you have taken the advice of someone who is.

I have not attempted to offer any advice about choosing your sporting support team in this section – I would fail my own golden rules if I did.

YOUR PROFESSIONAL ASSOCIATION/INSTITUTE

Whatever help or advice you are looking for, your first call should be to your local association/institute representative.

Athlete/player organisations in the UK are generally excellent. They provide an outstanding resource and help a huge number of people – their desire to do the best for their members is unquestionable.

I have already set out the wide range of benefits and assistance available, so I won't repeat myself by listing them again here. Suffice it to say that they are always keen to help.

As is often the case, money plays a big part – the better funded the association is the better it can look after its members.

But at the end of the day, it doesn't matter how wide the range of benefits is, or how good the services might be, if you don't make use of them. These associations can only do so much – you need to be pro-active and make the best use of what they have to offer.

So contact your local representative and ask them how they can help you.

ACCOUNTANTS/TAX ADVISERS

It is vitally important that your tax and National Insurance affairs are set-up correctly and that your annual tax return (if you need to complete one) is submitted accurately and on time.

Most sports pros will have access to basic advice and guidance through their local association/institute representative e.g. UK Sport have set-up a specialist web site for their athletes giving information on tax etc.

If you need additional help or on-going support, then your association/institute can provide you with a list of approved, specialist accountants and tax advisers. Importantly, they have experience and expertise in dealing with professional sportspeople.

How to choose a good accountant/tax adviser

How to go about choosing the right accountant or tax adviser depends very much on what it is you want and expect them to do for you.

The first thing to remember is that accounting firms are all different. Each firm will have a different style, offer different services, have expertise in different sectors and have different strengths and weaknesses – just like any other business.

Accountants can also provide a wide range of services from basic bookkeeping to specialist business advice. Some offer a full service, whilst others only focus on a narrow range, or may be specialists in one particular field.

It's vital that you choose an accountant who's experienced in dealing with professional sportspeople. Also, you need to be confident that your accountant can not only provide the help and support you need, but that they will do it in the way you want.

For example: Do you want to have as little as possible to do with your accountant – using them only to submit the documents you can't complete yourself? Or do you want an accountant who will give you proactive advice and perhaps be involved in developing a post-sport business?

Initial selection:
Put together a shortlist of at least two, preferably three or four accountancy firms. The easiest way of doing this is to ask colleagues, your club, association or institute, even friends and family, for recommendations.

Meet all the accountants on your shortlist and find out about their experience and services. This is also an opportunity for you to outline your needs.

Check whether you will be charged for this meeting. Most reputable accountants offer the first meeting free of charge

What to ask:
There are many questions you could ask, some can be fairly general, whilst others may need to be very specific to your situation and requirements. Here are some broad categories which should help you decide on the accountant who would best suit your needs.

Experience
Does the accountant have professional sporting clients and can they deal with your unique needs?

It's also worth finding out about their professional qualifications, background and expertise.

Charges
Few people like asking about fees and costs, but it's vital that you understand how your proposed accountant will charge right from the outset. Get a likely annual fee for comparison and for your own budgeting purposes. Ask some detailed questions about what their fees cover and whether they offer all-in/fixed fees. If it doesn't seem clear to you, ask again and make sure that you understand what is included and what is not.

People:
It's important to find out who will be handling your business on a day-to-day

basis – will it be a partner or someone more junior? Ask too, about the practice in general and get some background information, such as how many partners and employees the firm has.

Communication and service

You will be sharing some of your most important information with your accountant, so this is an ideal opportunity to find out about how they propose to work with you – and you with them. Ask about opening hours and check how easily you can contact them and whether they guarantee to get back to you within a certain period.

It's also vital to ask whether their service will be proactive e.g. will they remind you when you need to submit accounts or tax filings, or send you updates on changes in legislation that affect you?

Added value

At this stage, you may only want a simple service, but as your career develops you may perhaps need access to other services. So ask about the additional services they offer? For example; advice and help with starting a business.

If you're not sure what you might need in the future, ask how they think they could help you.

References!

Last, but certainly not least – get other clients' views of the practice to see if what you've been told is accurate. A good accountant should also be happy to pass on names of clients for you to take up references.

What information will they need?

Any potential accountant should want to know as much about you as you do about them. If you can take as much information as possible about you it will help both of you during your meeting.

Remember, it's a two-way conversation – you both want to get something from the meeting. Make notes as you go along – it is easy to forget things.

The following information will be useful – this is a guide, you may not be able to provide all these items:

- Background about you and your situation.
- Last tax return and, if applicable, set of accounts.
- What you are looking for from an accountant.
- Other support that you may require.
- Specific concerns or issues you may have.
- Timescale for any work you require.
- Any future business plans.

Making your decision
Once you've met all the accountants, it's time to make the decision. Take account of both your initial deciding factors and anything new that came up in the process. Don't be embarrassed to phone or email them with further questions after the meeting – after all, you are going to give them your business.

The key deciding factors are likely to include the following:

- Who best addresses your needs?
- Who do you think best understood you and your requirements?
- Which firm best meets your budget criteria?
- Empathy – which firm do you feel you can build the best relationship with?

At the end of the process, you should be in a position to choose an accountant – someone with whom you can develop a long-term relationship that will make this element of your financial life easier.

CHOOSING A FINANCIAL/INVESTMENT ADVISER

Whilst much attention has been focused on the mis-deeds of financial institutions in recent years – and the enormous harm they have caused – little has been said about the positive role that "good" financial advisers play.

In my view, there is no question that "good" financial advisers help to increase individual prosperity – and as a result, the prosperity of society as a whole.

People achieve greater monetary success, and as a result, they gain more control over issues within their personal and professional lives – *if* they get "good" advice.

But, do YOU need a financial adviser? And if so, how do you choose a "good" one?

Do you need an adviser? (And can you afford a good one?)

It may be that your affairs are relatively straight forward and, as a result, an adviser isn't going to be able to add much value.

Even if you are considering the kind of issues on the Financial Plan Health Checklist e.g. saving, pensions, insurances, tax planning etc. unless your affairs are sizeable enough, the cost of getting professional advice may be prohibitive, or deliver insufficient benefit to justify the cost.

There is a lot of information available now, especially on the web. If your affairs are relatively modest or straight forward then there is no reason why you can't do your own research. If you still want some professional advice then you could just pay for some initial pointers and perhaps for someone to look over your plan before you implement it.

But once your affairs get more complex, or the sums involved reach a "de – minimis" level, then there is no doubt that you will benefit from having a good adviser on board – someone with a proven track record of managing money successfully. After all you are talking about making big decisions that will affect your financial future – this is one area where "ok" is not acceptable.

The right advice will do far more than just help you with your general financial planning and investment portfolio. It will stop you making expensive mistakes; often based on ill-informed or emotional decisions – because it is often not what you know, but what you don't know, that "gets you." An experienced adviser will have the breadth of knowledge and expertise to highlight issues that you might not even be aware of.

You will benefit from having someone you can trust – help with assessing options – the provision and management of a structured, logical plan – and someone who will provide a counter-balance whenever your emotions threaten to drive your financial decisions.

Financially you should also be better off – a good adviser will endeavour to leave you in an improved financial position after all their costs and fees.

Jules Renard

"I finally know what distinguishes man from other beasts: financial worries."

And, perhaps above all, you will benefit from peace of mind. Knowing that you have someone you trust who is actively, enthusiastically and passionately looking after your best interests can deliver immense psychological benefit.

But, the attainment of these benefits is dependent upon you working with a "good" adviser. As with all professions, there are indeed many excellent people out there. But there are also a lot who won't deliver anywhere near the same level of value – and they don't all wear white loafers.

You need to be able to tell the good from the not so good because the cost of poor advice will often be far greater than just some wasted fees. You are playing for your financial future here – so choosing the right coach is absolutely critical and a decision worth taking some time over.

How to choose a good financial adviser

You want to ensure that your adviser operates in a manner that will always put your best interests first – without exception.

"Fiduciary – a person bound to act for another's benefit."

So how do you choose the right financial adviser for you?

Adviser remuneration
This is crucial because the way some advisers are paid creates a serious conflict of interests and is often found to be the primary driver behind poor or substandard advice.

For decades the financial services industry earned colossal sums in commission by selling products – this sales orientated culture resulted in many people receiving poor advice. Whilst commission was banned on the sale of all retail investment products from 31st December 2012 (still payable on insurance), this has not put a stop to opaque and sometimes excessive charging practices.

You employ an adviser for their expertise, their advice, their analysis and perhaps their organisational and administrative skills. Here is my financial life – please make it as effective and efficient as possible. But you need to make sure that what you want them to do is actually what they are doing – as in my experience there can be a gap between what the client thinks the adviser is doing for them and what he/she is actually delivering.

Of course you will have to pay for advice, but this charge should be clearly agreed up-front (in £ – not just %) – "a fair fee in return for a fair service." And you should always be aware of exactly what you are paying your adviser – if you are employing one on an ongoing basis make sure you know what you are paying each year.

A good adviser will always discuss remuneration openly with you and look to agree a fair fee for a clearly agreed level of advice/service. If they do not mention how they propose to get paid, or worse still, try and convince you they are providing a free service, walk away. If they cannot be honest with you about this issue, how can you trust them to look after your financial affairs?

Structure and clarity
Not all financial advisers work in the same way, or offer the same advice or service – there are huge variations and you need to sample these differences if you are to secure the one that best fits your personal taste and requirements.

Ask your adviser candidates to explain their initial and on-going service proposition – they should have these written down and readily available. If they are unable to demonstrate that they operate in a systematic and structured manner walk away.

Qualifications

Many advisers are general practitioners holding a range of qualifications (to varying levels of achievement), and offering a broad-based service to a wide-range of clients. Others specialise in one area of business e.g. pensions, or a particular client niche e.g. professional sportspeople.

If you want advice about a specific issue there is a strong argument to seek out an adviser that both specialises in clients like you, and whose experience and qualifications cover the issues of most importance to you. But a good generalist is better than a poor specialist.

If you want more holistic advice then look for someone who has a depth and breadth of knowledge that spans the insurance, financial, investment, legal and taxation disciplines. A good financial planner will often act as the conductor to your financial orchestra – co-ordinating the work of your other advisers (e.g. accountant and solicitor), to produce a Financial Plan that brings together every aspect of your finances to deliver the most effective and efficient result.

Of course, he/she won't be an expert in every field but a good adviser will know what issues require attention for a particular client, and know enough about those areas to seek expert, specialist advice when required.

Big versus small firms

Many financial advisers in the UK work for small firms, not large institutions. In the past you could have argued that a small practitioner couldn't offer the same quality of advice and service that a big firm could, but that simply isn't true anymore (if it ever was).

Technology has levelled the playing field and even the smallest practice now has access to the same tools, systems and capabilities as the largest global player. A one-man band can now, genuinely, provide you with at least as good a service as a well-trousered account executive in the sports division of XYZ private bank. They will almost certainly be cheaper too.

Unlike advisers from big firms, he/she will also be the one that makes the big decisions – not just the bearer of advice conjured up by a department you will never meet. And importantly, they are likely to stick around longer than advisers from large firms who have a great propensity to leave, or get promoted.

Judge them by the questions they ask you

Perhaps one of the most important indicators of a good adviser (whatever their field of expertise), is the questions that he/she asks you. Whilst they will need to collect a fair amount of factual information, they should be asking a lot of questions that really get you thinking.

Voltaire

"Judge a man by his questions rather than by his answers."

Rapport is important

Any client-adviser relationship is also just that – a relationship. And for it to work you need to be able to get on with and, most importantly, be able to trust your adviser. The best adviser-client relationships tend to be professional (of course), but also based on a foundation of mutual respect and friendship.

So, just as you would for any other job vacancy, don't just meet one potential candidate – interview at least two or three. This will not only provide you with a much greater choice of personality to choose from, but it will give you an invaluable insight into the many different service propositions out there – you will probably be surprised at just how different they are.

Speak to existing clients

Finally, speak to his/her existing clients – ask for a list of clients that fit your profile and then call a few. You don't just want to speak to someone who has been a long-term client, as they have obviously stayed because they like the service. Ask for clients who have recently signed-up, within the last couple of years, because they are best placed to tell you about the journey you are about to embark on – what was good and not so good – what they would do differently (if anything) if they were choosing an adviser again.

Finding a good adviser

So where can you look for a financial adviser?

Recommendations

Well, recommendations are a great place to start. Most people would rightly consider using someone that has been recommended by someone whose judgement they trust. After all, if they did a good job for X surely you wouldn't go too far wrong if you used them too?

Possibly, but don't be lazy and sign up to such an important, personal, and long-term relationship purely based on a 2-minute conversation with a friend or colleague.

Just because they rate this person highly does not necessarily mean that you will too – people's priorities, needs and standards differ and what one person values highly does not automatically mean the same to someone else. It is also possible that they are, in fact, not quite as brilliant as the referee thinks they are; or perhaps they do meet their needs well but they wouldn't deliver the same level of benefit to you.

Club, association, agent or management co. recommendation

In their drive to provide the most comprehensive service possible, player associations and agents will often forms "links" and "relationships" with providers of specialist services.

Whilst these can often provide routes to quality, vetted advisers, these "recommendations" are not always unbiased; nor do they provide any guarantee that these firms are the best or most appropriate people to help you. Often they are sponsors, or a big name – sometimes friends, or people they have some sort of (financial?) relationship with.

Of course, do speak to these recommended advisers, but also ask around and find a couple of alternatives you can interview as well. Apart from a bit of time, seeing a few advisers before choosing one to work with, doesn't cost you anything – but it could make all the difference in the world. And it could make you more informed on decision making.

Use the internet
There are quite a few websites that allow you to search for, and compare local advisers. I think three of the best are:

http://www.unbiased.co.uk/
A site that allows you to source all sorts of professional advisers (investment, pension, mortgage, tax, property, insurance and business), by specialism, qualifications and area.

http://www.vouchedfor.co.uk/search-for-ifa
A search site purely for reasonably qualified financial advisers – many of whom display endorsements from their existing clients.

http://www.financialplanning.org.uk/directory
The Institute of Financial Planning is the professional organisation of choice for some of the UK's leading advisers.

Summary

In summary, you must dedicate the time and effort needed to choose the right adviser and to providing them with sufficient time and information to enable them to advise you properly.

Regular contact will then ensure that he/she is kept fully informed of any changes in your situation, aims and preferences, so they can factor these in and ensure your financial and investment plans remain suitable and efficient.

Don't be lazy and just hire the first adviser you see – get a second, a third and even a fourth opinion. All it will cost you is a little time, but the benefits could be huge!

AGENTS AND PLAYER MANAGERS

Player agents are an inevitable part of professional sport and they do have a role to play. They can certainly deliver value but that does not mean every pro needs an agent and that any agent will suit any pro.

The first question you should ask yourself is: "Do I really need an agent?" What exactly are you expecting them to do for you and are you sure you can't do that yourself?

There are many examples of pros appointing an agent without having any real idea of what they are going to do, or whether they can really deliver value for money. Some just don't have a realistic chance of adding any meaningful value for that pro, at that time in their career. I have heard of pros who employed an agent as some kind of status symbol – you would think they could have thought of something more worthwhile to waste their money on!

Appointing an agent should be a commercial decision. The pro should be the boss and the agent their contracted employee – there to deliver a clearly agreed service in return for a specified fee.

Agents do have, potentially, a lot to offer.

• They can have a better understanding of a pro's value in the market place, which is useful when negotiating contracts.
• Their negotiation skills/tactics might deliver a better outcome than the pro would achieve themselves.
• They often have a lot of contacts, sometimes with specific clubs.
• They know about contracts and what is reasonable and what isn't.
• Increasingly their value is in negotiating sponsorship, endorsement and appearance deals.
• Some have media experience/contacts that you might be able to benefit from.

If it is just a matter of negotiating a good contract then you might want to speak to your association first. Many will have the experience and knowledge to assist and advise you – some will even negotiate contracts on your behalf. After all, if you are going to pay an agent 10-20% (and therefore only be left with 80%), are you really going to be better off using one?

If you are thinking of appointing an agent you need to go about this important decision in a logical and structured fashion. You need to think about how you are going to source a "good" agent and what you need to know about agents' contracts and what these should include and not include.

The world of the agent, whilst more organised and policed than it once was, is still mainly self-regulated. Yes, there are often checks in place and professional organisations run official registration schemes, and wield the ultimate sanction of disbarring those found guilty of breaking their regulations. But, as with all businesses, there are good and there are not so good people working within it.

Word of mouth is a great way of sifting the proficient from the ineffective – so speak to fellow players, especially the older ones who have more experience in this area. Also, talk to your professional association as it will often have a lot of good advice available.

When you talk to prospective agents, don't just let them talk, ask them probing questions about their business. The aim is to find out exactly what value they can deliver for you.

- How big is it – one-man band or big company? There are potential advantages and disadvantages to both – you must, however, challenge any statements to ensure there is substance and real value for you behind any claims.
- Are they full-time agents, or is this a second job? Just because it isn't their full-time occupation doesn't mean they won't do a good job but you might want some reassurance as to the level and quality of service you will receive.
- How many players do they manage? How much time and effort can they realistically spend on you? Where do you really stand in their list of priorities? It is one thing signing an agent who has lots of top pros on their books, but if you are not at that level is he/she really going to give you the attention you want/need/deserve?
- What clubs do they have contacts with? Are they ones that could be potentially useful/interesting to you?

- What media and/or sponsorship/endorsement contacts do they have? What could they potentially do for you in this regard?
- How are they remunerated and who is responsible for paying them? You want to pay for results and don't think that just because the club is paying that the money hasn't come out of your pocket.
- What other important issues can they help you with that you can't get via your club/association/institute?

There is a variety of choice when it comes to agents, but getting the right one for you isn't just a matter of picking the first one you come across, or the person you get on with. If you want to get the most from your agent you need to choose wisely – the difference might never become apparent, but it could be significant.

LOCKER ROOM EXPERTS

One of the greatest resources at your disposal is freely available and won't cost you a penny (well, maybe the odd drink). Your peers, especially those older, more experienced professionals, have a wealth of knowledge that most of them are usually more than willing to share.

Andy Caddick, Somerset and England Cricketer

"Be a sponge – learn from others. The best players absorb everything; have the guts to try different/new things and figure out what works best for them. Don't discard anything, regardless of whether you think it is relevant at this moment or not. Take it all on board as it will probably be relevant at some point."

Yes, I appreciate it can be especially difficult for younger pros to relate to anyone more than a few years older than themselves – it can be a bit like taking advice from your parents. But, the fact is that you can gain a lot and it would be remiss of you not to tap into their experience.

Think about it logically – if you want to make the most of the opportunities on offer, you firstly need to know what those opportunities are and also how to get yourself in a position to take advantage of them. But perhaps more importantly, you want to avoid making too many mistakes; or at least minimise the impact of those you do make. And what better way of finding out what those potential pitfalls are than by asking those who have gone before you and probably made quite a few of those errors themselves!

However, not all peer advice is good advice. In fact some of it can be dangerous – because people tend not to question it. Remember the golden rules of advice.

For example, beware of what I call the "Las Vegas" syndrome – people who are keen to tell you all about the great investment decisions they have made. It is just like asking people in the departure lounge at Vegas airport just how they got on in the casinos – the vast majority will tell you about their big winning hand, but very few will mention their losses, or the fact that they lost money overall.

Often, you can tell you are getting good advice because that person caveats what they say with something like "but you will have to think what will be best for you." It shows they have your best interests in mind and want you to think before you act.

But perhaps the golden rule is to remember you are not seeking advice on "what you should do", but rather that you are after some help clarifying the main issues so you can make an informed decision yourself. You should always assess how any information you gain is relevant to your own, personal circumstances before deciding on a course of action.

FRIENDS AND FAMILY

Friends and family can be a hugely important resource.

They most likely know "you" the individual (as opposed to you the athlete), better than anyone else. And they may be more willing to be honest. They are probably not directly involved in your sport – which can be a bonus, as they will see the bigger picture. They may also have skills and experience which would be valuable to you e.g. business experience, legal or financial expertise etc.

But they are also human and you need to remember the golden rule when considering advice from any source – if it is something this person has experience with, or is a proven expert in, then "ok"; but if they haven't, then don't act until you have spoken to someone who has.

GET YOUR VARIOUS ADVISERS TO SPEAK TO EACH OTHER

The best advice will ensure you achieve your objectives effectively and efficiently.

The best advisers combine experience, knowledge and an ability to consider the big picture. You cannot deal with financial issues in isolation and the best theoretical/exam answer is not always the best solution for every client.

People matter; often some of their needs are intangible and it is their evaluation of success that counts, not the adviser's.

The difference between good and average advice can be substantial but often difficult to assess without an in-depth knowledge of the subject yourself.

A healthy dialogue between your various advisers (legal, financial and tax), will ensure they share ideas, discuss options, keep each other informed and achieve the best, co-ordinated outcome for you.

When choosing a new adviser, or evaluating the performance of an existing one, getting a second, third or even fourth opinion will provide you with the information you need to make an informed decision. The worst that can happen is you confirm you are doing the right things; at worst it will show you where your planning is deficient.

CONCLUSIONS

You should now understand why having a Financial Plan is so important.

You now know what issues your Plan should cover and why.

You can review your current debt position and draw-up a plan for non-mortgage debt repayment.

You now have some appreciation of the psychology behind good and bad savings habits. You can assess what level of savings you should (and could) be making – and put the necessary things in place (e.g. direct debit instructions), to ensure it happens regularly and automatically.

You need to review the retirement benefits being provided by your club and/or association – and compare these against your own needs. Identify any shortfall in provision and make plans for additional pension investment.

You must consider where your finances are vulnerable due to a loss of income from long-term injury, illness or death. Take out suitable insurance to cover any unacceptable risks.

If you don't already have an accountant, or tax adviser, draw-up a list of several candidates and arrange to see them.

Consider the financial and logistical position should you die. Contact a specialist solicitor and arrange to have a will drawn up, if you haven't already got one in place.

Consider your sources of support and advice – and make the best use of those resources available to you.

EXERCISES – KEY IDEAS – ACTIVITIES

1. Put together your own Financial Plan – starting with your aims and goals.

2. Identify any priority issues/areas and tackle these first.

3. Take it one, manageable stage at a time.

4. If you have non-mortgage debts – prepare a repayment plan and put it into action.

5. Work out what you should (and could) be saving and get a direct debit in place to ensure this amount is saved automatically each month.

6. If your club/association pension arrangements are insufficient for your needs, get advice on the best way to top this up.

7. Would you, or your family, be in financial trouble if you were injured, ill or dead? If so, work out what the risks are for you and get specialist insurance advice.

8. Ensure you have a will in place and that your affairs are in order – just in case.

9. Plug into as much support and advice as you can – but use it wisely and prudently.

NOTES

HOW TO SUCCESSFULLY INVEST YOUR LONG-TERM SAVINGS

Investment "success" means different things to different people. But many savers reduce their chances of achieving success by investing poorly.

Darren Baker, The Author

"The financial cost of a poor investment plan can sometimes be difficult to calculate, but the consequences can be grievous and life-changing."

Investing is a complex and highly specialised subject. To do it properly requires experience and specific expertise – even many financial advisers are not investment experts.

So why, if it is such a complex subject, is it important that you at least know the basics?

1.   Because if you don't know anything, you will never be able to make an informed decision – whether that is evaluating your adviser's advice or validating your own thought process.

2.   Without some basic understanding, the likelihood is that you will make poor decisions that will lose you money.

3.   Investing is not a win-win game – there will be times when the value of your savings fall. Knowing a bit about what you are investing in, and why, will do a lot to alleviate your concerns when this happens…

4.   … and stop you making bad decisions when they do fall.

INVESTING – THE COLD, HARD TRUTH

In the last 25 years I have only met a handful of people who "really" knew how well their investments had performed. Gut instinct is often about as accurate as it gets.

But surely this information is essential? What have you, as an individual investor, actually made in £ profit (or loss), after you take into account all of your various transactions and deducted all of the associated costs? And how did that compare to what happened to asset prices in general?

The investment industry rarely provides investors with such transparent and personalised information. What it usually proffers instead is generic performance figures, over meaningless time periods (i.e. not over the actual time that person had invested), and before the deduction of all the costs and fees that investors have to pay. The most publicity also tends to be reserved for those funds with the best performance – with statistics carefully chosen to be as impressive as possible. Smoke and mirrors!

So what is the true story and how can you accurately track and compare the performance of your own investments?

The truth about investment returns

In July 2007, Lukas Schneider published a paper which compared UK stock market returns with UK stock market "investment fund" returns, with UK stock market "investor" returns. Lukas's research mirrored analysis already carried in the US (Dichev 2007; Nesbitt 1995; Friesen and Sapp 2006).

The 3 questions he asked were:

1. What was the performance of the UK stock market over the period in question?

2. What was the comparative performance of funds that invested in the UK stock market over that same period?

3. What returns did the average UK stock market investor actually achieve?

All of these studies reached the same, broad conclusions.

1. The average investment fund under-performed the asset they were investing in by a statistically significant margin – in this case they under-performed the UK stock market.

2. That the "pocket to pocket, money-weighted" return actually enjoyed by the average investor was statistically lower than the return achieved by the average investment fund.

The graph on page 107 shows a simplified summary of the conclusions of Lukas's research.

The exact figures are not important; it is the difference between them that requires attention.

These conclusions were not revolutionary – many existing studies had separately produced the same results. This was, however, the first time all four aspects had been compared together using UK data.

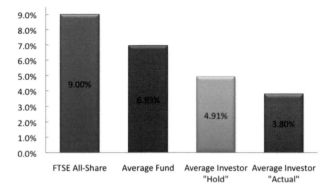

- The *average fund* under-performed the UK market in which it was invested by about 2% per annum. See section "5 – Build your portfolio" later in this chapter.

- The *average fund investor* would have under-performed the average fund by a further 2% per annum, IF THEY HAD BOUGHT AND HELD THE AVERAGE FUND OVER THE ENTIRE PERIOD – the loss mainly a result of fund charges and trading costs.

- The *average UK investor* however, DID NOT BUY AND HOLD THE SAME INVESTMENT, but instead bought and sold several times during that period – often as markets went up and down. This trading reduced the actual return achieved by the *average UK investor* by a further 1.11% per annum. See section "2 – Getting your head straight."

So what are the lessons we all need to learn here?

1. The average "active" investment fund under-performs the market. So you need to take great care in choosing which funds you invest in – see "5 – Build your portfolio."

2. Costs and charges matter – they can take a significant chunk out of your profits.

3. Buying and selling in an attempt to try and "time" your investment i.e. buy low and sell high, does not work. No-one has ever been able to do this successfully/consistently and the net result of this practice is likely to be a further reduction in your investment returns.

"Wraps" and investment admin accounts

It is virtually impossible to keep track of the real performance of your investments without some electronic help. This is one of the advantages of using a "wrap" or investment admin account, as these systems automatically keep track of all the pertinent data. I have covered these in the "Reviewing Your Financial Plan" section of the Performance chapter.

HOW TO INVEST SUCCESSFULLY

To invest successfully you need to employ a logical, structured approach.

Warren Buffett

"To invest successfully over a lifetime does not require a stratospheric IQ, unusual business insight, or inside information. What is needed is a sound intellectual framework for making decisions and the ability to keep emotions from corroding that framework."

The investing process I use with my clients centres around five basic steps:

1. **Set long-term investment objectives.**
   Set objectives for your savings that are appropriate for your timeframe – and your willingness, ability and need to take risk.

2. **Getting your head straight.**
   It is vital that your investment decisions are based on fact – not emotion or as a result of fancy marketing. Take some time to understand how to make good investment decisions – and avoid making bad ones.

3. **Assessing your attitude towards risk and volatility.**
   This is vital as your attitude to, and willingness to accept risk and volatility, will determine the "asset allocation" i.e. the type of things you should invest in and the amount that you should invest in each.

4. Plan your asset allocation.

THE most important decision when it comes to investing. You need to decide how much of your portfolio to invest in each of the different investment types, or asset classes, including stocks, bonds and short-term investments, both domestic and foreign.

5. Build your portfolio.

With an asset allocation in place, you can now construct a portfolio suited to your needs, goals, investment horizon and risk attitude. Your goal is a diversified portfolio investment that will maximise your return potential, whilst minimising risk.

1 SET YOUR LONG-TERM INVESTMENT OBJECTIVES

So what is it that you are saving for? For many of us our ultimate dream is to achieve financial independence – the ability to fund our desired lifestyle without having to work to provide an income. But we all have other things that we want out of life, for example a house, car, holidays – possibly a hobby or passion that we want to indulge. If you have children then you may have additional goals such as private or university education, or helping with house deposits and weddings.

Some of these things may be way into the future – and that can be a good thing. Because one of the many surprising facts about investing is that having a long horizon is a powerful advantage. You want your horizon to be as long as possible, because as an investor, time is your best friend.

The simple fact is that the more time you have, the more likely you are to succeed as an investor. Why? There are two reasons. The first is the miracle of compound growth, and the second is the phenomenon of risk reduction over time.

The miracle of compound growth

Compound growth operates on a very simple principle. When you put money aside to earn returns, and then reinvest those returns, you have both your original investment and the returns working for you. The longer you allow this process to continue, the greater your accumulation will likely be.

Imagine putting £1 million into an investment that consistently earns 8% every year. The table on the next page shows how the compounding process works.[2]

YEAR	STARTING AMOUNT	EARNINGS	ENDING AMOUNT
1	£1,000,000	£80,000	£1,080,000
2	£1,080,000	£86,400	£1,166,400
3	£1,166,400	£93,312	£1,259,712
10	£1,999,005	£159,920	£2,158,925
20	£4,315,701	£345,256	£4,660,957

Risk reduction

Time actually helps reduce risk, especially when it comes to investing in things like shares. It is natural to worry that if you invest in the stock market today, it may go down tomorrow. But if you have a long investment horizon, tomorrow is just one of the thousands of market days during which you will be investing. Over long periods of time, many of the ups and downs in the market are cancelled out, leaving the broad market trend.

The graph on the following page shows how the annualised returns for the FTSE All-Share UK Index (main UK stock market), narrows as your horizon becomes longer. It shows results based on the performance of the FTSE All-Share Index[3] from Feb 1955 to Dec 2012.

The UK market, like all world stock markets, has produced a wide range of outcomes. An investor holding stocks for just one year could have had returns ranging from a high of 151.4% to a low of −55.84%. Investors with longer

2. Figures are for illustrative purposes only and are not a guarantee of future performance. Figures do not reflect the effect of fees or taxes.

BEST/WORST RETURN FTSE ALL-SHARE UK INDEX (FEB 1955 – DEC 2012)

Annualised Average Rolling FTSE All-Share	1 Year	3 Years	5 Years	10 Years	15 Years	20 Years
UK Index	14.01%	12.76%	12.52%	12.60%	13.22%	13.74%
Best Return (Start)	151.41% (Jan '75)	56.52% (Jan '75)	36.06% (Dec '74)	31.62% (Jan '75)	27.71% (Jan '60)	23.02% (Apr '89)
Worst Return (Start)	-55.84% (Dec '73)	-26.12% (Jan '72)	-10.58% (Jan '70)	-0.68% (Mar '99)	1.25% (Jan '60)	6.94% (Apr '89)

horizons face much less volatility. An investor with a twenty-year investment horizon could have experienced returns ranging from a high of 23.02% per annum to a low of 6.94% per annum.

Until the crash of 2008, no investor with at least a ten-year time horizon would have achieved a negative return. However, anyone who invested in the FTSE All-Share in March 1999 would have experienced a return of -0.68% per annum over the next ten years. And that is before you factor in the additional "real" value loss due to inflation.

2 GETTING YOUR HEAD STRAIGHT

There is a very good reason why we are encouraged not to talk about money, religion or politics at dinner parties – these topics stir up our emotions and acting upon our emotions can result in poor decision making.

Benjamin Graham "Security Analysis", 1934

"The investor's chief problem – and even his worst enemy – is likely to be himself."

There are four main Darwinian compulsions that you need to be aware of:

- Fear and greed.

- Belonging and acceptance.

- Certainty vs. uncertainty.

- Fiction vs. fact

This powerful combination has done more damage to more people's savings than any stock market crash.

How we feel about something has a profound influence upon whether we actually decide to do it, regardless of whether or not we know it is in our best interests to do so. Example – it shouldn't matter when you transfer some of your wages/income into savings, but most of us find it much easier when it is done immediately and automatically. As soon as we have to get involved, make a decision and then act, somehow it all seems so much harder to do.

But even after you have done the hard part and put some money aside, emotion can ruin things when it comes to deciding what to invest in and when.

1. Fear and greed

When things are going well, people naturally want to push the limit – take a few more risks when risk taking seems to be paying off. Conversely, when things go badly, people just want the pain to stop, often regardless of the cost.

But it is often when things look at their best that they are about to start going wrong; and when things look bleakest that turns out to be the best time to invest. If you followed your emotions though, you would end up buying investments at their top price (on the basis they had performed so well recently and you wanted some of that) and selling out when assets are worth their least e.g. right after a market crash!

The Emotional Rollercoaster for Investors

And the investment industry targets these emotions very effectively. They will often promote a fund that has performed well recently, because they know people will invest in it.

James Goldsmith

"If you see a bandwagon, it's too late."

But, all investment assets are cyclical, sooner or later this fund's performance will reverse, it will fall in value, and people will sell it in favour of the next "big thing" – actively encouraged by an industry that generally makes a % every time you switch.

The fact is that your heart is a pretty awful judge when it comes to investing; often happy to act on little more than hope, hype or a good sounding story – or simply the desire not to have to think about something boring/worrisome any more i.e. investing. Your brain, on the other hand, has the ability to make well thought out decisions based on evidence and logic.

This is why it is vital to remove emotions from all investment decisions. Making decisions based on emotions – emotions probably triggered by extreme event(s) – will more often than not result in poor decision making and this can easily lose you money and sabotage the achievement of your goals.

So what is the answer?

"Discipline, structure and process."

By establishing a clear, logical and evidence-based investment process you will not only give yourself the best chance of investing prudently from the outset; but you will also find it easier to avoid making costly mistakes along the way; and easier to keep on track when your emotions try and take over – "No, let's stick to the plan!"

2. Belonging and acceptance

The basic human instinct for "belonging" and "acceptance." In other words, if your peer group appears to be making a fortune from the latest hot stocks, you not only feel that you are missing out (greed) but also that you are not one of the in-crowd (acceptance).

The loss of "bragging rights" in the golf club bar has thus tempted many otherwise rational investors to abandon sensible, long-term diversified strategies in favour of short-term gratification which they later repent at leisure. Or perhaps not at leisure – as their retirement plans are postponed because their investments have failed to perform.

Any investor who finds themself challenged in this way should take comfort from the mathematics underpinning the concept that consistency beats volatility and that a well-diversified "boring" portfolio will beat the "exciting" hot stocks over the long-term.

	CONSISTENT INVESTMENT		VOLATILE INVESTMENT	
YEAR	RATE OF RETURN	END VALUE	RATE OF RETURN	END VALUE
1	8%	£108,000	30%	£130,000
2	8%	£116,640	-20%	£104,000
3	8%	£125,971	25%	£130,000
4	8%	£136,049	-20%	£104,000
5	8%	£146,933	25%	£130,000
Arithmetic Return	8%		8%	
COMPOUND RETURN	8%		5.39%	

Returns on a single premium of £100,000 invested at the beginning of a compounding period.

3. Certainty vs. uncertainty

Human beings are hard-wired to crave certainty over uncertainty – but there simply is no such thing as a sure thing when it comes to investing.

There are, of course, a lot of very talented, intelligent people working in the financial world and some are definitely better than others at what they do. There has never been anyone however, who has been able to predict the future with any degree of consistency. No-one can regularly pick out the next big company, sector or economy for you to invest in; whilst avoiding those that will lose you money.

In fact, study after study has shown that the people who get it right one year are just as likely to make the wrong bets the next year as they are to continue their winning streak.

Beverley McLean, "The Sceptic's Guide to Mutual Funds"

"The truth is, as much as you may wish to know which funds will be hot, you can't – and neither can the legions of advisers and publications that claim they can."

You only have to listen to any economic or investment programme to realise that many so-called financial experts are second only to politicians when it comes to saying a whole lot of nothing, very convincingly. And put two or more financial gurus in the same room and each will give you a whole boatload of excellent sounding reasons as to why the other is just plain wrong.

One of the ways investment professionals convince people to invest is by showing them past performance figures i.e. the historic returns "they missed out on." But all investment assets are cyclical – none of them rise consistently every year; but rather enjoy periods of growth *and* periods where they either don't rise in value, or fall. Be wary of anyone who encourages you to invest in anything by simply quoting past-performance figures.

The problem is that people tend to see what they want to see and some people want to believe they have found that next big investment opportunity – or have found someone who has. Those people are either very lucky or just plain kidding themselves.

4. Fiction vs. fact

"Facts are stubborn things, but statistics are more pliable."

You need to be on your guard as advertisers and advisers know exactly what buttons to push.

William W Watt

"Do not put your faith in what statistics say until you have carefully considered what they do not say."

What about the financial press? Yes, the papers are full of articles written by "financial journalists", but some of these have little or no "on the ground" experience or formal qualifications. What they do have though is enormous influence over large audiences who understandably believe that they are gurus. The same can be said of some TV broadcasters.

Obviously there are a lot of journalists and broadcasters who are knowledgeable and present important information in an interesting and accessible way – but it is working out who is worth paying attention to that is the problem. Even I get a headache trying to wade through all the "investment pornography" to find the small amount of unbiased, useful stuff.

Then there is the financial industry, a business famous for performance related pay – not dished-out on "how well they do for their customers", but according to "how much money they can make for themselves" – see the conflict of interests?

The marketing departments of financial companies spend huge sums trying to make you believe that their businesses are the most trustworthy, secure and profitable one for you to invest your money with. Of course they do – it is their job and they are often very good at it.

The majority of information entering the investment arena is generated by the active fund management industry (stockbrokers, fund groups and financial advisers) and transmitted by the financial media in its many forms.

The former have a considerable vested interest in propagating the myth that they are the best, as their primary function is to gather people's assets under their management and justify the high fees they charge. As for the latter, their main purpose is not to educate the investor, except in the most superficial way, but to generate advertising revenue from the active fund management industry.

But how can you, a lay-person, sift through the "spin" and work out what facts are relevant and unbiased? And how can you then put it all into context and make informed decisions without years of experience and expertise?

The simple answer is that it is very difficult. The good news is that a "quality" financial adviser knows that the over-whelming proportion of investment and economic information out there is little better than "white noise" – and can help by sifting through it all for you. A lot of it just seems like it should be important (and the media will generally tell you it is – where's the story otherwise?), when in fact it is nothing more than a distraction.

This is one of the big positives that comes out of having an on-going relationship with an adviser who acts on a fiduciary basis i.e. they are paid to look after your financial best interests – not sell you products. By providing structure and explaining what you are doing and why, they can help you ignore worrying, stressful or titillating financial news and enable you to get on with living your life.

3. ASSESSING YOUR ATTITUDE TOWARDS INVESTMENT RISK AND VOLATILITY

When it comes to investing, one of the most important questions you need to answer is "what sort of risk taker are you?"

Mark Twain

"October is one of the peculiarly dangerous months to speculate in stocks. The others are July, January, September, April, November, May, March, June, December, August and February."

Psychologists have shown that we feel loss about twice as keenly as we feel gain. So when you are considering what investments to make it is not the potential upside that you should be concerned about, but the potential downside.

Nearly every investment carries an element of risk. And whilst most people are happy to accept that as fact, what a lot of people don't realise (or seem perfectly willing to ignore when it suits them), is that:

"Risk and reward are related."

The return, or potential return, of every investment works on this simple principle – although it may not always be that obvious.

Regardless of what anyone tells you, if an investment has the potential to generate higher returns than are available from a risk-free cash deposit account (one offered by a highly-secure provider), then without doubt, it also carries greater risk.

This basic risk vs. reward principal applies to any asset that you could possibly invest in – businesses (stock markets and corporate bonds), governments (bonds, gilts), property, currencies and commodities.

The more risk, the greater the return "potential" must be because no reasonable investor is going to be interested in investing in it otherwise. To attract investors riskier assets have to offer at least the chance of higher returns – whether that is greater interest or dividend rates, or the potential for greater capital appreciation. But they are also not going to pay any more than they need to either!

This all makes sense, doesn't it? It seems pretty straight forward to me, but time and time again I have come across intelligent, experienced investors who have lost money in a scheme that promised high returns with "low or no risk."

"If it is too good to be true, then it probably is."

Sometimes it was a "clever" scheme e.g. one that used complicated stock market techniques to multiply the potential returns whilst only risking a small amount of the original investment capital. Sounds good doesn't it, but I have yet to find an investor who really knew how these schemes worked – never, ever invest in something you don't fully understand.

DIFFERENT TYPES OF RISK

"What is the definition of "Broker?"
The person you trust with thousands of your hard-earned pounds. Hello!"

When people generally think about financial risk they think of losing money.

Sure, losing money is something you need to consider carefully.

1. Risk – that you might lose some, or all of your money.
2. Risk – that your investment grows but by less, after all costs and taxes, than

the rate of inflation. *(This means that although your money may go up in value, it does not grow sufficiently to maintain its "real" spending power e.g. your money grows by 2% in a year but inflation is 4% over the same period – net result is that your money is worth 2% less than it was the year before).*

3. Risk – that you choose the wrong investment, or mix of investments, and as a result your savings do not grow as well as they could/should have.

But there are also other, perhaps less obvious types of risk that you also need to consider.

YOUR ATTITUDE TOWARD RISK

While you can do a great deal to mitigate risk, you cannot eliminate it. In any investment plan, it is important to understand both the types and the amount of risk you are taking and to be sure that you are comfortable with these. This understanding will greatly increase your ability to adhere to your long-term investment plan and increase your chances of achieving your financial goals.

The right level of risk for you depends on both your personal preferences and your situation. I break the risk equation into the following four parts.

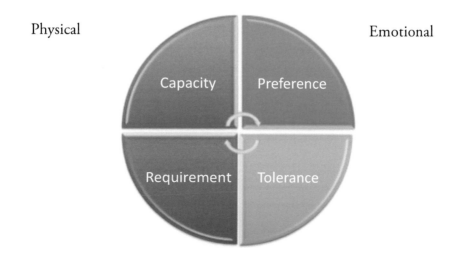

1. Risk Preference: Your Own Preference to Investment Risk

The amount of risk that you think you want to take – the level of risk you think you would be comfortable taking.

2. Risk Tolerance: Your Emotional Response to Market Fluctuations

Over the course of your investment life, the value of your portfolio *will* rise *and* fall. Equity markets, in particular, are very volatile and investors must expect that there will be regular periods of rising prices *and* regular periods of falling prices.

Your risk tolerance describes your level of comfort in waiting through the downturns. If the risk you take is within your risk tolerance, then you will be able to maintain your investment strategy through both strong markets and weak ones, giving you the best chance of investment success.

To put it another way, Risk Tolerance represents how you are likely to react when a risk turns out badly.

3. Risk Capacity: Your Financial Vulnerability to Losses

Your tolerance for risk may be high, but as a prudent investor, you should consider your ability to withstand financial losses. Because market downturns are unpredictable, you need to assess the real economic harm you might face if your portfolio seriously declined in value.

4. Risk Requirement: Your Need to Take Risk

Most investors would not choose to take more risk than is necessary. But if you need your portfolio to grow more quickly over your time horizon, you will want a higher rate of return. An increase in your rate-of-return objective, however, will generally mean taking more risk. If your risk requirement is higher than your risk tolerance or your risk capacity (your vulnerability to losses), then you must adjust one or more of these parameters. This could mean retiring later; subjecting yourself to the discomfort of greater risk; or increasing your savings.

On the other hand, if your rate-of-return objective can be lowered because your assets can support your goals with less growth, then your need to take risk is reduced and your portfolio should be allocated accordingly.

DECIDING HOW MUCH RISK YOU WANT AND NEED TO TAKE

The right level of risk for you depends on both your personal preferences and your situation.

For example, if you were just about to invest some money which option(s) would you prefer:

1. **A Bank/Building Society investment that guaranteed a gross return of 3% per annum, fixed.** *Expectation – the rate of inflation is likely to be higher than the after tax return from your bank/building society account, so the "real" value of your money will fall by between 0.5-2% each year.*

2. **A balanced investment portfolio that is predicted to produce annualised returns of 8% over the long-term, but actual annual returns could be anywhere within -15% and + 25%.** *Expectation – long-term this portfolio should deliver average annualised returns of 8%, which should be higher than inflation so your money will rise in value. But you have no guarantee of this and you will have to accept a level of risk and volatility along the way.*

3. **A penny share tipped in a specialist magazine.** *Expectation – some previously tipped shares have risen in value by 50-200%, but at least as many have fallen substantially in value, or have even gone bust, losing their investors everything.*

The above is an overly simplistic way of looking at risk. For most of us the answer will be a mixture of 1 and 2 (possibly with a small amount gambled on 3 for a bit of fun).

But over the longer-term you can't afford to keep too much in cash as the net returns are likely to be lower than inflation, which means the "real" value of your savings will fall. So you need to invest long-term savings in assets that

THE RELATIVE RISK PROFILE OF SOME COMMON INVESTMENT ASSETS

Spread betting
Options

New share issues
Penny shares
Unregulated investment schemes

Small cap or value shares
Emerging markets

Large and mid cap shares
Actively managed share funds
Share tracker funds

Balanced actively managed funds
Balanced tracker funds

Corporate bonds
Gilts & government bonds

Cash deposits

VERY HIGH RISK

HIGH RISK

MEDIUM RISK

LOW RISK

The above table is for indicative purposes only. It is vital that you assess the exact risk profile of any investment before you commit to invest any money.

download

*You can download this and many other useful resources by visiting our "toolkit section" at **www.yourfinancialcoach.co.uk/toolkits***

have the potential to out-perform inflation. This means investing in a portfolio that contains equities – the exact amount of which will depend upon how much risk you are able/willing to take.

Risk profiling tools

In the "old" days, people's attitude to risk was often assessed in simple and often meaningless ways. "How would you rate your attitude to risk?" – "Medium?"

Well, most people say medium, but the fact is that everyone's definition of medium is different – I know my brother wouldn't touch a curry I rated as "medium!"

These days there are various tools professional advisers use to gauge the risk profile of their clients. One of the most commonly used is the "Investment Risk Questionnaire."

Risk profiling questionnaires can provide a useful means of gauging people's attitude towards investing, risk and loss. They ask lots of clever questions – and by cross-referencing they check to see if there are any areas of ambiguity that need to be explored further.

Whilst a good start however, a good professional will always go further than a simple questionnaire. One of the best ways to gauge the right level of risk for someone is by getting them to look at the historic returns achieved by various risk-rated portfolios. This way they can "see" what risk actually meant and what extra returns, if any, they would have got for taking-on that additional risk.

Looking at the historic returns achieved by portfolios will also prepare you mentally for the inconsistent returns you are likely to get – especially for the years when you will make very little, or even lose money.

4. PLAN YOUR ASSET ALLOCATION

Asset allocation is the process of deciding how much of your portfolio to invest in each of the different investment types, or asset classes – Cash, Bonds (or Fixed Interest), Property and Equities (Shares).

Asset allocation should be your first investment decision because it is the most important.

To investigate how important asset allocation really is, three leading American investment experts performed a comprehensive statistical study to measure the importance of various factors in determining a portfolio's performance. They studied a broad range of portfolios over widely varying market conditions. Their conclusion was that, on average, 94 percent of the variability in returns of a given ten-year portfolio could be explained by the asset class selection policy being used (see chart overleaf). The balance of the profitability was attributed to the policies of individual security selection (4 percent) and market timing's buy and sell decisions (2 percent).[4]

Determinants of Investment Portfolio Profitability

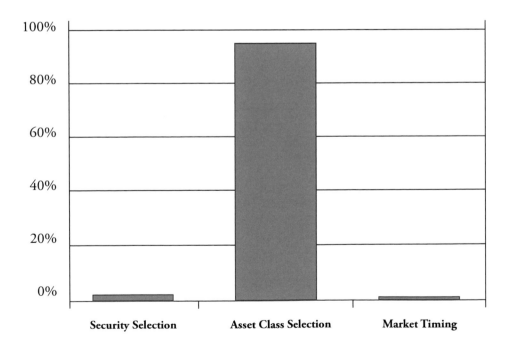

THE FOUR BASIC INVESTMENT ASSET GROUPS

1. **Cash** – An account at a banking institution that allows money to be deposited and withdrawn by the account holder.

2. **Bonds** (Fixed Income) – A method used by companies and governments to raise capital. Bonds are bought by investors in return for a promise from the company/government to pay regular interest, and to repay the loan at a specified time.

3. **Property** – An investment made in land and/or property. This can either be done directly, or via companies or investment funds that invest in property.

4. **Equities** (Shares) – The buying and holding of shares in a company in anticipation of income (in the form of dividends) and capital gains, as the value of the share rises.

THE EQUITY (SHARE) – BOND (FIXED INCOME) DECISION

The choice between shares and fixed income is a clear example of the basic investment trade-off between risk and return.

You can see overleaf that, historically, equities have far outperformed fixed-income securities. For example, one pound invested in common stocks (as represented by the UK All-Share Index) at the beginning of 1955 would have been worth £630.15 (assuming reinvestment of dividends) by the end of 2012. That same pound invested in UK Treasury Bills would have been worth £55.03. Investments over this period required an increase in value to £22.96 simply to maintain purchasing power (to stay even with inflation).

Cash Flow Growth Chart

Monthly: 02/1955 - 11/2012; Default Currency: GBP

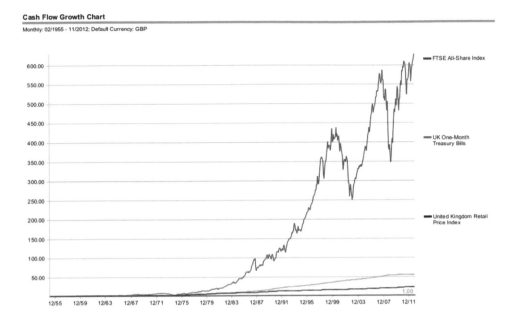

UK Stock Market February 1955 – December 2012[5]

Based on this information you might understandably think: "Heck, I'll put most of my money in the stock market." But look again at the big falls – the lengthy periods when you would have lost a substantial percentage of your investment; and experienced negative returns over many years. What affect would such prolonged losses have on your financial position and the achievement of your goals – let alone your nerves?

So, how do you confidently allocate between stocks and bonds?

A risky portfolio holds 100% stocks, and the least volatile portfolio holds 100% bonds. Between these extremes lie standard stock-bond allocations, such as 80%-20%, 60%-40%, 40%-60%, and 20%-80%.

---

5   For the fifty-seven years from 1956 to 2012, the compound annual growth rate of return was 11.79% for the UK All-Share Index, 7.18% for UK Treasury Bills, and 5.57% for UK Inflation (RPI).

HYPOTHETICAL PORTFOLIOS
50 Years – Jan 1, 1963 – 31 Dec 2012

	Fixed	Defensive	Conservative	Moderate	Aggressive	Equity
Equity	0%	20%	40%	60%	80%	100%
Fixed Income	100%	80%	60%	40%	20%	0%
Annualised Return (%)	7.1%	8.5%	9.7%	10.7%	11.5%	12.1%
Annualised Standard Deviation (%)	2.8%	4.1%	6.7%	9.5%	12.5%	15.5%
Growth of £1	£30	£58	£101	£160	£250	£306

Standard deviation is a measure of volatility. About 68% of the time annual returns will be within 1 x standard deviation of the average annualised return (e.g. If the average annualised return = 9.7% and the standard deviation = 6.7%; then 68% of the time the annual return will be within 3.0% – 16.4%). Two standard deviations would account for about 95%. The wider the range of returns the more risk there is in the investment portfolio.

Assumes annual portfolio rebalancing and includes fund TERs and an assumed 1%pa adviser management fee. The above figures are provided for illustration purposes only and should not be construed, in any way, as recommended investment strategies. Past performance is no guarantee of future results.

As suggested in the risk profiling section, by looking at the historic returns achieved from a range of portfolios with different Bond/Stock mixes you can choose one which during major market crashes e.g. 1974, 2002 and 2008, didn't fall by any more than you could handle without panicking and cashing-in your portfolio. And remember, at the time these crashes happened, all the news was bad – you certainly weren't feeling confident that it was all short-term and markets would bounce back again anytime soon.

Bond/fixed income strategies

There are two main reasons why you hold fixed income in a balanced investment portfolio:

1. To reduce the overall volatility of your savings or;
2. To generate a reliable income stream.

These objectives can lead to different investment decisions.

The first, volatility reduction, uses fixed income to temper portfolio instability. Rather than trying to maximise yield from your bonds, you hold them primarily because they are lower risk.

Most long-term investors would be best served by taking this approach – investing more in equities if you want to increase potential returns. In this case, you are better off investing in high-quality, short-term bonds – which may have a lower yield, but are far less volatile.

The second reason for holding bonds is to generate reliable cash flow. Income-orientated investors such as pension funds and trusts may not worry as much about short-term volatility in their bond portfolio. Their priority is to meet a specific funding obligation in the future. Consequently, they accept more volatility in the hope of earning higher yields, which they pursue by holding bonds with longer maturities and/or lower credit quality.

Whilst higher yields sound attractive, various academic studies have shown that the volatility of such bonds is almost as high as equities – whilst the total returns (income and capital) they produce are less. On a total return basis therefore, you would be better off investing in higher-quality, lower-yield bonds and investing more in equities where you get properly rewarded for the risks you take.

Whether investing for total long-term return or for income, a portfolio should be diversified across issues and global markets to avoid uncompensated risk from specific issuers and to capture differences in yield curves around the world.

Refining your equity allocation

After establishing your basic share-bond mix, you can turn your attention to refining the equity allocation, which is where the best opportunities to improve the risk-return trade-off are found.

The tendency can be to go for a home market bias – with a large proportion of the shares being UK companies. But the UK market represents only 8% of the world stock market and by holding an array of equity asset classes across domestic and international markets; you can reduce the impact of underperformance in a single market or region of the world. This diversification can reduce volatility in a portfolio, which translates into higher compounded returns over time.

If you are comfortable with higher doses of equity risk you can overweight or "tilt" your allocation toward riskier asset classes that have a history of offering average returns above the market. Research published by Eugene Fama and Kenneth French found that small cap stocks (smaller company shares), have had higher average returns than large cap stocks, and value stocks have had higher average returns than growth stocks. By holding a larger portion of small cap and value stocks in a portfolio, you increase the potential to earn higher returns for the additional risk taken.

Summary

The equity-bond decision drives a large part of your portfolio's long-term performance. Evaluating different combinations can help you visualise the risk-return trade-off as you consider the range of potential outcomes.

And as your appetite for risk shifts over time, you can revisit the mix to ensure it remains appropriate for your changing needs.

THE EFFICIENT FRONTIER

Optimal or efficient portfolios are theoretical concepts and are achieved when a portfolio provides a maximum mathematical return for a given level of risk. In order to determine these efficient portfolios it is necessary to analyse every combination of assets and plot the expected risk-return outcome for each combination. The optimal or efficient portfolios are then defined as those which maximise the expected return for the desired level of risk.

Having established the expected outcomes for all the combinations of assets, a line can be drawn to join up each of the optimal portfolios at each risk level; this line is known as the Efficient Frontier. This is illustrated in the diagram below.

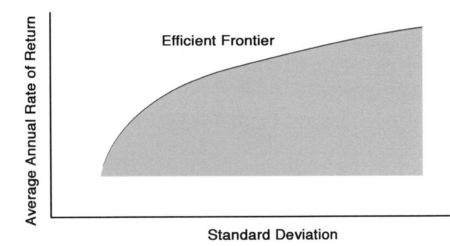

There are no portfolios with better theoretical risk-return profiles than those plotted on the Efficient Frontier.

Your, or your adviser's, objective therefore is to design a portfolio that will place you at your optimal point on the efficient frontier.

EXAMPLE 60% GROWTH – 40% DEFENSIVE PORTFOLIO

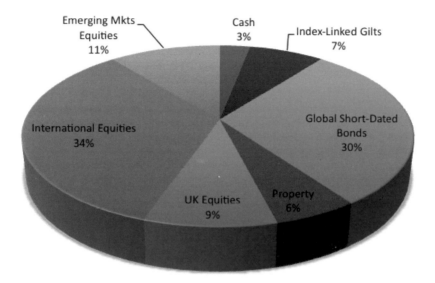

As you can see, 40% of the total portfolio is allocated to less volatile, defensive assets (cash, Global Short Dated Bonds and Index-Linked Gilts); whilst 60% is allocated to UK and Global Equities and Property.

The above portfolio is for illustrative purposes only and should not be taken as any kind of recommendation. You should always seek independent advice from a suitably qualified professional – and ensure any investment is appropriate for your needs and attitude to risk.

5. BUILD YOUR PORTFOLIO

Once you have settled on the asset allocation for your portfolio you can choose what fund(s) to buy.

You can either pick out individual funds for each asset class that you want to hold, or you could opt for funds that hold a range of assets e.g. managed/balanced funds.

Buying individual funds

This is undoubtedly the best way to ensure you are always invested in the assets you want – that your portfolio always has the risk profile you want – and that the underlying charges are as low as possible.

There are basically two types of investment fund that you can buy: "Actively" managed and "Passive."

Actively Managed – The fund manager will try and beat the market they are investing in by: i) buying stocks they hope will go up in value and selling stocks that they think are about the go down; ii) timing when they trade – trying to buy low and sell high. An example would be a UK Equity fund that tries to beat the performance of the FTSE All-Share Index.

Passive (Index/Tracker) – A fund that simply tries to emulate the performance of an asset class e.g. A UK All-Share Index Tracker fund that mirrors the performance of the UK All-Share Index.

Now at first glance, you might think "Well, I'll go for the Active fund – at least they are trying to out-perform." However:

Active fund managers spend hundreds of millions of pounds each year trying to derive some competitive advantage, so that they can beat the market. However, the net result of this activity, which is ultimately paid for by investors in higher management and transaction fees, is that not only does it not *add* value; it is more likely to *subtract* it. In other words – the vast majority of active funds DO NOT outperform.

In fact the evidence that most Passive/Index/Tracker funds beat most Actively Managed funds is compelling and endorsed at the highest levels. These funds are also cheaper – meaning you capture more of the available returns and keep more of them as well.

In my view Passive/Tracker/Index funds are the better choice – effective, efficient and cheaper.

Buying managed/balanced funds

Rather than build a portfolio from component funds that invest in individual asset classes, it is tempting to opt for one that invests in a suitable mix of assets e.g. a managed or balanced fund.

Managed funds can indeed offer a reasonable option but they do have several potential drawbacks. The manager will have the discretion to alter the fundamental mix between defensive and risky assets. This will be within a reasonable range, but it could mean that you find yourself with a portfolio that is riskier, or taking less risk, than you want. They will also be free to invest in whatever assets they choose – and this will change depending on their view of markets etc. Managed funds will also always be, by their very nature, actively managed – so the charges will probably be higher than a passive alternative.

Costs and charges matter

It is very important that you minimise your investment costs and charges – after all they are coming out of your pocket.

There are 3 potential costs:

1. Advice – your financial/investment adviser.
2. Investment Funds – the costs and charges incurred by your investments.
3. Custody – administration costs e.g. a portfolio, or wrap account.

It is important that you are aware of all the costs – including the hidden ones. For example, an investment fund's "Annual Management Charge" might be 0.75%pa; but when you include other costs like dealing charges, its "Total Expense Ratio" (TER) might be 1.0% – you pay the 1%!

The total costs of investing will depend on what advice and service you receive, but total costs for a full investment management *and* financial advice service should not exceed 2%pa – any more and you should question whether you are actually going to be better off.

REBALANCING PORTFOLIOS

Rebalancing is the means by which you maintain a consistent risk exposure. For example, after a prolonged bull market the balance of equities and fixed income in your portfolio might have shifted from 60/40 to 70/30 – leaving you more exposed to the downside than you are prepared for.

Although rebalancing is a simple concept, realising its benefits is a challenge for many investors because it involves selling assets that have recently done well and buying assets that have recently done poorly in order to return to the original allocations.

However, understanding that over the long-term performance tends to be mean revert (i.e. periods of above average performance are followed by periods of below average performance), rather than maintain upward or downward trends indefinitely, should help you overcome any reluctance to do what appears to be counter-intuitive – i.e. sell some of a successful investment rather than hold on to all of it.

Rebalancing has been proved to increase portfolio returns with no additional cost in terms of risk. However, it is not an entirely 'free lunch' as, in order to rebalance, some transactional fees and expenses may be incurred.

The key is to set a rule as to when and why the portfolio will be rebalanced and stick to this rule e.g. if the holding in any assets is +/- 5% from its target, then action is taken to correct this imbalance.

ALTERNATIVE INVESTMENT ASSETS

In the hunt for bigger and better returns some people turn to more exotic investments. The usual suspects being: hedge funds, private equity funds (venture capital etc.) and commodities.

Others like the idea of investing in a more tangible asset; something they think they understand – property.

How are these different from the traditional asset classes that I have recommended in this book? Should you include alternatives in your portfolio?

Some reasons given for considering alternatives

A common argument for including alternatives is that they have a good return potential and a low correlation with traditional asset classes i.e. they don't move in tandem.

While it is true that many alternatives are not highly correlated with standard investments, this fact alone is not sufficient to justify adding them to your portfolio. For example, a bet on the outcome of a weekend football match has no correlation with stock market returns, but that doesn't mean betting on sports should be part of your investment strategy!

There is little evidence that alternatives have higher returns than traditional asset classes. Personally, I am not convinced that many investors, advisers (or even managers if the banking crisis is any indication), fully understand the risks they are taking. Often alternatives include one or more elements that increase risk: they borrow money; make concentrated bets; trade excessively.

And exclusivity, whilst possibly creating an aura of mystery and attraction (human nature), doesn't necessarily mean higher returns. Many hedge and private equity funds have high minimums that put them out of the reach of most investors, but there is no evidence that they deliver greater rewards than traditional assets classes – whilst the risks are often much larger. "Fund of funds" programs do allow access to such funds at lower minimums, but the additional layer of administration simply adds further costs; making the net value of such arrangements questionable. Personally, I would never invest in "funds of funds."

HEDGE FUNDS

Hedge funds come in numerous guises and follow an extremely broad range of investment and trading strategies. I will therefore not attempt to do anything here apart from provide the most general of overviews.

You often hear about hedge fund managers earning millions for themselves and extraordinarily good returns for investors. However, there are just as many (if not more) examples of extraordinarily bad results and even the implosion of high profile hedge funds.

The lack of persistency in the performance of hedge funds is about the same as that of traditional active managers. The chance that a hedge fund that outperforms one year, will outperform again the next year, is only about 50%. This is what you would expect by random chance.

Before you even consider hedge funds you need to understand that they are often higher in cost, less diversified, more leveraged, and less liquid than traditional investment funds.

PRIVATE EQUITY INC. VENTURE CAPITAL

Private equity invests in companies that are either private (not publically traded on the stock market), or will be taken private (through the buy-out of a publically traded company). Often they do this using relatively small amounts of equity investment and large amounts of debt. Venture capital, as the name suggests, usually targets start-up or early development companies that are riskier and may not have much in the way of real assets.

Successful firms add value by getting involved in the management of the company, to help drive greater efficiencies and growth. The objective is to sell the business for a multiple of its original acquisition cost, usually through a stock market floatation, purchase by another company, or recapitalisation (when the business borrows and repays its owners.) But this is usually at least 5-7 years into the future – often more.

As with hedge funds, it is very difficult to provide any meaningful assessment of the performance of the private equity industry. There are certainly some spectacular success stories – as well as many disasters. Trying to differentiate one from the other at the outset is a lottery.

Private equity investments are often higher in cost, less diversified, more leveraged and less liquid than traditional investment funds.

COMMODITIES – METALS, ENERGY, AGRICULTURAL AND TIMBER

Commodities include natural resources such as agricultural products (grain, food, meat etc.), precious and industrial metals (gold, silver etc.) and energy (gas and oil). You can invest in commodities in a variety of ways such as through investment funds, futures contracts (bets on the future price of a commodity), exchange traded funds, or direct ownership (often impractical).

Advocates argue that commodities serve as an inflation hedge and some assets (usually gold), provide a safe haven in times of stock market distress. But historic data shows that commodities are more volatile than stocks, and their returns do not always rise with inflation because of this significant volatility. Potential investors should also consider the economic argument against holding commodities. Unlike stocks, commodity futures do not generate earnings or create business value. They are essentially a speculative bet in which there is a winner and loser at the end of each trade. Moreover, a broad-based stock portfolio already has significant commodity exposure through ownership of companies involved in energy, mining, agriculture, natural resources, and refined products.

PROPERTY

I don't know whether it is the British love of property, or the plethora of property development programmes on TV, but investing in property seems to be an option that many professional sportspeople consider. But just because you might have the financial means to buy property, does not mean it would be a good idea for you to do so.

Including a minority property holding (e.g. 5-10%), as part of a portfolio is one thing – it provides a useful diversifier, without impacting greatly on the total expected returns. But investing in property on a large scale, in addition to your principal private residence, is something completely different altogether.

Property development, renovation – call it what you like, is not an easy business. Despite what many people seem to think, there are not lots of run-down houses out there that will yield a good profit for the investor who dabs on a bit of fresh paint and puts in a new bathroom and kitchen.

In my experience, most people who "try" property development make very little, if any money at it. For countless reasons they usually find that their initial budgets bear little resemblance to the final cost and unforeseen delays mean the eventual sale is finalised many months later than expected.

If you are considering property renovation, or development, don't do anything until you have done a huge amount of research. Speak to people who have a proven track record in the area, and with the type of property you are thinking of buying.

Preferably work for a building renovation company for a while. Not only will you pick-up, or improve, your own skills, but you will begin to understand how a building site works. This invaluable insider knowledge will help you make better decisions, gain the loyalty of your contractors, minimise delays and additional/unforeseen costs, and save you tremendous amounts of stress.

Perhaps consider financing a builder with a proven track record, rather than being hands-on yourself. Obviously, ensure you have a solicitor draw up a suitable contract that will protect you and your investment if you do this.

Buy to let – whether combined with a bit of development or renovation, buying property to rent it out is another common option that many people consider. I often hear people say things like: "I can buy this house for £X and rent it out for £Y – that is a 5-6% yield and will easily pay off the mortgage and provide a bit of income as well."

But this is not the whole picture. There are obviously costs involved in buying and selling property – and these will come out of your "profit." The rent is also taxable, so you need to subtract tax at your marginal rate. Yes you can put costs against your tax bill, but these are unlikely to be significant in most years. You may decide to employ a professional letting firm (10-15% of rent), and you will have to maintain the property – which means general on-going maintenance and redecoration. You are also not guaranteed a tenant (let alone a good one) – so there may be times when you are getting no rental income at all, whilst still having to pay council tax.

Perhaps the biggest issue landlords complain about is bad tenants – some of the stories are horrendous. Yes, you might be lucky, but generally people don't treat other people's property as carefully as they do their own.

Many professional property owners that I know estimate that they often have little rental income left after all costs and taxes have been deducted. The majority of any "profit" therefore, is often down to a rise in property values – and as I write this the next property boom seems some way off. And even if you do sell for a profit, you will have to pay Capital Gains Tax on any net gains above your annual allowance (if it is not your principal private residence).

Summary

Investing in alternative assets can be profitable, but for many people this option represents nothing more than a "white elephant" – at best providing a distraction; and at worst costing them money.

My belief is that you don't need to invest alternative investments in your portfolio to have a successful investment experience; particularly considering their higher costs, lack of diversification, and liquidity constraints.

If you are going to invest in alternative assets or property do your homework and make sure you really know what you are doing before you invest.

SOMETIMES THE BEST DECISION IS TO DO NOTHING

The "DO NOTS" of investing are as important as the "DO's."

I appreciate why people sometimes just want to do something as they feel that taking some action must surely be better than doing nothing. But making mistakes when investing can result in serious, long-term financial damage and perhaps put you in a situation from which you will never be able to fully recover.

Common sense is a great, instinctive tool that you should listen to when investing – if something doesn't feel quite right then don't do anything unless, or until, your concerns are fully addressed.

The following list is not exhaustive, but hopefully you will see a common theme running through it.

Don't:

- Invest in something about which you have only had a verbal explanation – get the recommendation in writing and then spend some time thinking about it before taking action.
- Invest to a deadline – never be rushed into making a decision. Very rarely is there a good reason why you should act within a certain timeframe.
- Invest without fully understanding what it is you are agreeing to. Even professionals struggle to understand some schemes simply because they are so complex (and many such schemes sounded great but ended up losing investors a lot of money).
- Invest without reading and understanding all the small print.
- Invest in anything that, if you sit back and think about it honestly, sounds too good to be true.
- Increase your mortgage and/or other debts to the maximum the lenders offer you – you will leave yourself vulnerable.
- Invest based on tips from the locker room, golf course or dinner party without checking with an independent professional first.

- Value your investments daily – if you have made the right decisions then they only need to be reviewed periodically and doing it too often will just drive you nuts and probably result in you making poor decisions.
- Trade investments regularly. Again, if you have the right investments you won't need to trade very often. Transaction costs can mount up and easily wipe out any small gains you might make.
- Invest in the next fad, craze or "big thing."

Be very careful when mixing relationships and money. People have different attitudes to money and mixing the two can easily result in problems.

FINANCIAL PRODUCTS AND TAX WRAPPERS

I have purposefully only provided basic background information on "Financial Products" in this book – and only then at the end of this chapter. This is mainly because the choice as to whether to use a product can be a complex decision and not one that can be covered properly in this format.

But it's also because I wanted to make the point that choosing a product or tax wrapper should be the last decision that you make – and even then you should only ever use one if it will somehow benefit you. This is often contrary to the way many people, and certainly many providers of financial services, seem to go about investing.

The bad old days

The old model of building an investment portfolio was completely upside down. Typically the adviser would select a suitable product (e.g. ISA or Pension) normally based on taxation considerations. They would then select a suitable provider based purely on product features and charges. Finally, suitable investment funds would be chosen from the selected provider's available list. As asset allocation is the single most important factor in the construction of a portfolio it follows that this should be the first stage in the process.

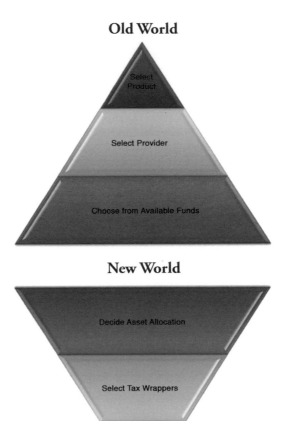

The old world methodology typically resulted in haphazard and poorly diversified portfolios that were very difficult to monitor and control.

The result has been that many people have been left with products that deliver little real, tangible benefit, whilst the underlying investments are left in expensive investment funds that fail to deliver decent returns (and in some cases actually lose a proportion of the investor's money!)

So my strong recommendation to you is, concentrate on getting your investment process right first, and then decide whether or not putting those investment assets in a tax wrapper or product would benefit you.

COMMON UK INVESTING VEHICLES

Here are some very basic descriptions of common UK investment products.

Unit Trusts, Open Ended Investment Companies (OEICs), Exchange Traded Funds (ETFs) and Investment Trusts

These are the most flexible type of product, allowing you to get your money out at any time. They can invest in a variety of assets e.g. shares, bonds, property etc. Some of them invest in a particular industry, country or region whilst others will invest in the whole market. They are also responsible for most of the colourful adverts in the weekend papers.

Unit Trusts.
A unit trust reduces your risk of investing by pooling your savings with thousands of others and then spreading it across a range of shares or other types of investment.

OEICs.
Open ended investment companies were introduced into the UK in 1997 – and are similar to Unit Trusts in many ways. Open-ended means shares in the fund will be created as investors invest and cancelled as they cash in.

ETFs.
A fund that tracks an index e.g. FTSE 100, rather than invest in a pool of shares managed by a fund manager. ETFs are traded like shares; are often more tax-efficient than unit trusts or OEICs and can have lower operating and transaction costs.

Investment Trusts.
Investment Trusts are companies that buy and sell shares in other companies. When you invest in an investment trust company, you become a shareholder of that company. Your shares will rise and fall in value according to supply and demand for the shares.

Pensions

See previous chapter.

ISAs

Strictly speaking an ISA is not actually an investment product, although it often gets confused with one. It is just a tax-efficient wrapper that sits around an investment such as cash, shares, or a unit trust/OEIC. How much tax, if any, you actually save will depend upon your tax position, the type of assets you invest in, and the amount of income and/or gains you realise.

You can invest £11,880 into an ISA during the 2014/15 tax year. Of this sum, £5,940 can be held in a Cash ISA, with the remainder in a Stocks and Shares ISA – or alternatively, the whole amount can be invested in stocks and shares. There is now also a junior ISA (JISA) for those under 18.

Investment Bonds

An investment bond is in fact a whole of life assurance policy, provided by an insurance company, and usually paid for with a lump sum (or single premium). There are both UK "Onshore" and "Offshore" versions – each with different tax implications.

Within the bond you can invest in a wide range of assets, but it is the tax status of these wrappers that potentially makes them useful tax planning vehicles. Capital withdrawals of up to 5% of the amount invested can be withdrawn each year without triggering an income and/or capital gains liability. An investor can therefore delay such liabilities until a time of their choosing e.g. perhaps when their income drops and they go from being a higher-rate tax payer to a basic rate taxpayer – thus limiting the tax liability to the basic rate.

Endowment policies

An endowment policy is a savings and life assurance policy for an agreed period. The minimum period is 10 years. A tax free benefit is normally paid out at maturity or on earlier death.

These products require you to commit to investing a regular amount over a long time. That's no bad thing in itself, but if you do not manage to keep up the payments you can end up losing out. "Qualifying" versions can potentially be attractive to higher-rate taxpayers, but their inflexibility, restricted annual contribution level, and often limited investment choice, mean that they are not often the best choice for investors.

Annuities

A conventional annuity is a contract whereby the insurance company agrees to pay to the investor a guaranteed income either for a specific period or for the rest of his or her life, in return for a capital sum.

CONCLUSIONS

You need to know a bit about investing because you are ultimately responsible for your investment success (or failure).

You need to approach investing in a structured, logical and disciplined manner – create a plan and then stick to it.

Understand the relationship between risk and reward – and why time is an investor's friend.

Appreciate how emotion and marketing can affect your decision making.

Evaluate your personal attitude towards investment risk and volatility – this is key when choosing what to invest in.

Asset Allocation is the most important decision you will make – you, or your adviser, need to get this bit right.

Choose funds that meet your asset allocation needs effectively and efficiently.

Keep costs and charges down – they can really eat into your profits if you are not careful.

Be wary of investing in alternative assets – they might sound exciting but they are often highly complex and you can easily lose a lot of money.

Property is a specialised area and not really suitable for amateurs. If you are considering property, then get expert advice and be prepared for a steep learning curve.

Always think before you act – remember the "don'ts" of investing.

Choosing a product or tax wrapper is the last decision you should make.

EXERCISES – KEY IDEAS – ACTIVITIES

1. List your investment goals, the timeframe of each and the funds you have available for investment.

2. Prioritise the list from 1 – allocate funds to each.

3. Qualify and quantify your attitude towards risk – how much could your savings fall in value before you would panic and sell-out?

4. Agree a suitable asset allocation for your long-term portfolio(s). This may be different for different goals e.g. riskier for longer-term goals and more defensive for short-term objectives.

5. Choose funds that give you the asset exposure you want effectively and for minimal cost.

6. Review your decisions to ensure they are rational, unemotional and reasonable.

7. Consider whether using a tax wrapper to hold your investments would yield any meaningful benefits – and for what additional cost.

NOTES:

CHAPTER THREE

PERFORMANCE

It is crucial that you are able to manage the competitive demands of your life both on and off the field, so that you can perform at the highest level possible.

Richard Bryan, Bath, Newport and Leeds – lawyer and RPA player development manager

"You need a financial plan and a plan for life after sport – these are important issues that you should be concentrating on. And ensure any advice you get is independent and of good quality."

As a sports professional you have to fit many aspects of your life into and around intensive training and competitive programmes. When striving for excellence it is often too easy to miss the bigger picture and ignore some of the fundamental aspects of life, and the fact that one day your sporting career will come to an end and you may have to change direction.

The career of an elite athlete is, at best, a short one and for those unfortunate professionals who suffer serious injury, it can be all-too-brief. Whilst a chosen few stay in the game, in a coaching, management or media capacity, the vast majority of professionals will probably have to earn their living outside the sporting arena.

But rather than use their time in sports as a platform to springboard themselves into the next phase of their life, some people remain completely focused on the here and now. The problem with doing this is that some goals simply cannot be achieved overnight – they require sustained effort over a prolonged period.

1. **FINANCIAL PERFORMANCE** – Making sure your finances are in good shape – after all, you will still have bills to pay once you retire from sport.

2. **LIFE PERFORMANCE** – Maximising your future career prospects – most of your working life will still be ahead of you after your sporting career is over.

Doing some prep work during your sporting career will put you in a much better position when you retire.

FINANCIAL PERFORMANCE

Having to give up professional sport will be hard enough – you really don't want to have money worries as well. And the fact is that your financial health can have a huge impact on your emotional well-being – so make sure it is a positive one. From a position of financial strength you will enjoy greater choice and more opportunities – and experience less stress and pressure.

There are going to be at least 2 main phases to your working life; maybe more. You need to ensure that your finances will be able to support your desired lifestyle once you retire from sport – and then continue to do so throughout the rest of your working life and into retirement.

Whilst you may have a pretty good idea of what financial rewards your sporting career may bring, have you considered the remuneration you could expect to get from your next job?

It is quite possible that your earnings during your sporting career will be the highest of your life. If that is the case, and if you want to maintain your lifestyle after you retire, you are going to have to use those monies earned from sport to subsidise your post-sport income.

Neil Jenkins, Welsh + British and Irish Lions International – now WRU Skills Coach

"You can't play forever so don't waste your money. Put some aside and obtain financial security for you and your family."

Obviously it depends on your individual situation, occupation, experience, qualifications etc. But a starting salary of £25-30,000 seems to be about average for professional sportspeople entering the commercial workplace for the first time. Would that be enough to finance your lifestyle?

Don't just live for today – be sensible and also consider tomorrow.

REVIEWING YOUR FINANCIAL PLAN

Hopefully you have followed the steps in the Preparation chapter and have now created your own Financial Plan – or at least the core of one.

If you have only had the time, inclination or attention span to tackle some of the aspects of your Plan, keep at it. Try and put a bit of time aside on a regular basis to work on the next step. Remember, the best way to eat an elephant is one mouthful at a time.

Good habits

Getting into good financial habits is perhaps the most important thing you can do. If you can also set-up your finances so that as much as possible is automatic e.g. regular savings; that will also help.

Pat Lally, PFA Director of Education

"Don't live to the limit of your finances. You need to look ahead and put some money aside for your future."

Make a diary note at least once a year to stop and think about your financial management; your habits (good and bad), and what you might be doing financially that is good, and what areas you need to work on.

Plan your reviews

Regular reviews are important and the only way to ensure that you remain on track to achieve your goals. Having a written plan, even if it is just a one-page summary makes this process much easier – and provides a very useful record of your progress.

Make a diary note to carry out a formal/detailed review of your Financial Plan at least once a year. Try doing this when you know you are going to be less busy e.g. off-season.

You might also want to review certain aspects of your Plan at particular times during the year e.g. tax planning at the end and/or start of each tax year. Breaking up your financial review into manageable parts can also help if you find dealing with it all in one go a bit much.

You should also review your Plan if something significant changes in your life e.g. pay rise, getting married, injury etc.

Try printing off your Financial Plan, or parts of it, and keeping a copy in your kit bag. You probably have times when you are sitting around for prolonged periods e.g. flights, coach, rainy days etc. and these can provide perfect opportunities to do a little reading/planning. I suppose the same principle applies to this book!

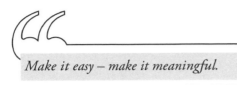

Make it easy – make it meaningful.

Get help/delegate

And get help with those aspects that require specialist/expert advice e.g. investments. A good adviser will also help you with your Financial Plan; highlight areas or issues that might require attention; do most of the legwork for you; and help keep your financial affairs effective and efficient going forward.

MONEY MANAGEMENT PROGRAMMES

It is crucial to keep track of your income and expenditure – regardless of how much you might earn; but especially if money is tight. It is amazing just how often people under-estimate how much they have spent, and on what.

Even if you earn a "decent" wage it is very easy to relax and spend far more than you planned too (or perhaps could really afford to.) Whilst not having to worry too much about money might be one of the benefits about having a healthy income, even the wealthiest people need to budget properly if they are to remain wealthy.

Money management programmes can make income and expenditure monitoring and budgeting much easier – especially when used in conjunction with on-line banking.

It only takes a few minutes to download an on-line bank statement and categorise each item. The reports these programmes can then produce are extremely powerful. At a touch of a button you can see what money you have had coming in – and where it has gone.

Typical money programme graphs

At a glance, graphs like these can tell you whether you are over-spending, as well as what you are spending your money on. If you want to investigate a particular aspect in more detail, a simple click will then list the bank entries behind that item.

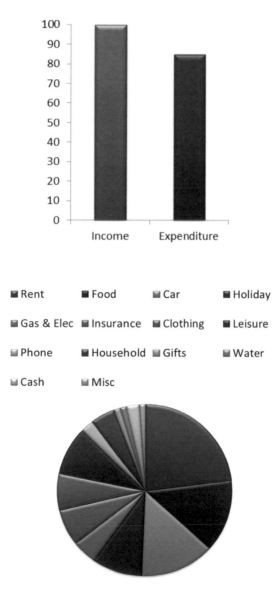

USING "WRAPS" AND PORTFOLIO ADMIN ACCOUNTS

In the "old" days, people used to buy a range of insurance and investment products from numerous providers. This usually meant that, after a few years, people lost track of what they had and why they had it. Keeping track of numerous investments can be difficult and time-consuming – so much paperwork and so little of it makes any sense!

Over the last decade or so the use of on-line portfolio accounts (investment, wrap accounts) has become more and more prevalent. These administration "platforms" enable investors to use one central account to hold numerous different investments, from many different providers.

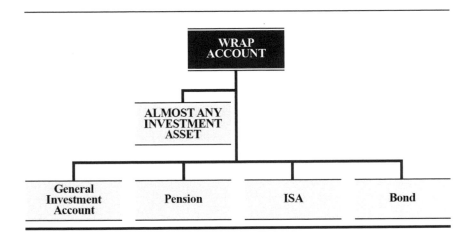

download

*You can download this and many other useful resourses by visiting our "toolkit section" at **www.yourfinancialcoach.co.uk/toolkits***

The most flexible systems enable you to buy virtually any UK recognised investment asset (share, Unit Trust, OEIC, Insurance Company funds,

Investment Trusts etc.) and provide a full range of products and tax wrappers to hold them in e.g. ISA.

Once the account has been set up, you can view and manage your investments on-line. Valuations, deposits, withdrawals, buy and sell instructions etc. can all be done electronically, which saves a lot of time and paperwork. This efficiency helps when it comes to transaction costs, which are often lower than those payable when dealing direct with investment providers. You also get access to investments that would normally be impractical, or impossible to buy by traditional means.

These accounts do charge – usually a percentage of the value of the underlying investment value and a small fixed charge for tax wrappers such as ISAs. You therefore need to consider whether the benefits are worth the additional cost – but using an electronic admin account can make a lot of sense if you have a number of investments, and/or are investing a reasonable amount of money.

LIFETIME CASH-FLOW FORECASTS

A big problem with planning for the future is that it is just that – the future. The human brain can find it extremely difficult to appreciate how changing a few numbers from the "spend" column to the "save" column today, for example, will yield significant and valuable benefits years from now. And if you can't understand it, how can you value it?

To try and bring such planning "alive", financial planners will often use "Lifetime Cashflow" software. These computer programmes run the numerous calculations required to provide a forecast of how your finances might look in the future.

Yes, such projections may be imperfect – based as they are on numerous assumptions about the future; many of which may well turn out to be wrong. However, it is better by far to have some method of validating your financial plan than simply keeping your fingers crossed that it will all work out fine.

Graphs demonstrate what your finances may look like in the future – income vs. expenditure – value of accumulated savings etc. And by changing a few of the underlying assumptions it can easily show you the future effect of making a few changes now e.g. how saving a bit more could strengthen your financial position upon retirement.

Lifetime cash-flows can make the impalpable tangible – a rare and valuable glimmer of reality in what is generally an incomprehensible and boring deluge of wordy plans, theories and numbers.

This probably doesn't look easy to understand. But once you know what information is driving the output, and what each section means, this type of financial forecasting can be extremely powerful.

A lifetime cashflow provides a constructive, visual representation of your financial plan – and a vital way of measuring whether you are on course to achieve your goals.

Even if your current plans are unlikely to be able to fund your future goals, at least if you have some prior warning you have a chance to change your current plans accordingly – or re-evaluate your future objectives.

For many of my clients the lifetime cashflow graph is the most valuable piece of paper I produce – and they will eagerly compare this year's version to last year's to monitor their progress.

Monte Carlo Analysis

Prepared For: ProSports   Prepared By: Your Financial Coach

1. Portfolio '60' Characteristics

Fixed Income Content	40%
Equities Content	60%

Geometric Return (Net of Inflation) %	3.50%
Arithmetic Return (Net of Inflation) %	3.99%
Risk % (Annualised Standard Deviation)	9.84%
Allowance For Expenses	1.72%

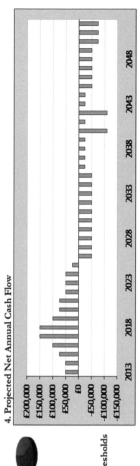

2. Probability of Falling Below 0%, 50% and 100% Thresholds

	£250,000	£125,000	£0
5 years	0%	0%	0%
10 years	0%	0%	0%
20 years	0%	0%	0%
30 years	10%	6%	3%
40 years	37%	31%	24%

3. Probability of Running Out of Money

5 years 10 years 20 years 30 years 40 years

4. Projected Net Annual Cash Flow

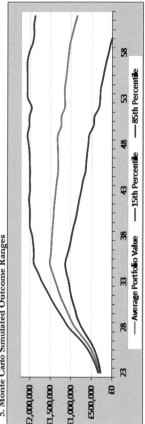

5. Monte Carlo Simulated Outcome Ranges

—— Average Portfolio Value —— 15th Percentile —— 85th Percentile

6. Potential 10 Year Capital Values (based on an initial investment of £250,000)

	Year 1	Year 2	Year 3	Year 4	Year 5	Year 6	Year 7	Year 8	Year 9	Year 10
85th Percentile	£336,512	£412,810	£518,694	£656,743	£848,868	£1,058,267	£1,197,860	£1,339,611	£1,474,224	£1,590,907
Average Portfolio Value	£307,032	£365,094	£451,325	£566,332	£731,561	£900,800	£1,021,650	£1,119,859	£1,223,057	£1,305,196
15th Percentile	£276,859	£317,643	£384,020	£476,173	£613,254	£745,303	£843,337	£901,407	£969,797	£1,019,941

LIFE PERFORMANCE

This section is all about "being released back into the wild" – the time when your sporting career ends and you ….?

Kevin Jones, Sports Division, Clarke Willmott Solicitors

"Players need to take the initiative and plan for their future."

The truth is that the life of a professional sportsman or woman is permanently on a knife-edge. Career threatening injuries can strike at any time and sporting 'form' can sometimes be as changeable as the weather.

Sportspeople are constantly under mental as well as physical pressure and there is rarely enough time to think about life after sport. What is often hardest for a sportsperson to come to terms with is being an 'ordinary person'. What can replace the adrenalin rush or the adoration of the crowd or, more importantly, the feeling of achieving personal success in a chosen field?

But you need to think wider than just today's training schedule and your next race/game/performance. Take those blinkers off and consider what you want from the next phase of your life – and what you need to be doing now in order to achieve those goals.

Tim Nicholls, Head of the RPA Player Development Programme

"Very few pros have an idea of what they want to do when they retire from sport. Our (RPA) main goal is to try and get players to plan ahead and especially consider issues such as qualifications and employability."

How long will your sports career really last at the top flight and what are you going to do afterwards? This is not always the same as what you would like it to be, or what you would like to do. What can you really offer the "real" world that it would find valuable – other than your name and fame?

The likelihood is that you do need to start planning now, even if the end of your sporting career is still, hopefully, many years off – perhaps so far in the future that it is really difficult to know what you want to do.

BUILDING BRIDGES

For many pros the end of their sporting careers is a difficult time in their lives. Many find it hard to adjust having been forced to stop what they love doing and unceremoniously thrust back into the "real" world to fend for themselves. And this all usually happens when they are still relatively young!

It can be much harder if you find your future employment options are limited because you have no skills or talents that are "marketable in the real world." Consider how you would feel if you had to exchange your fulfilling sporting life for a job that doesn't "light your candle" and/or doesn't pay very well.

Chloe Roddick – Horse Trainer and Point to Point rider.

"I have always run my own training business alongside my riding career."

You need to make sure that you have a back-up plan – something else going on in your life. Now, this might be sports related, but it has to be something that would be sufficiently useful to someone else so that you could earn a living from it – preferably also something that you enjoy doing.

Getting the work vs. life balance right

Every individual has talents, ambitions and priorities that are unique to them.

In order to choose a career/life path that is right for you, you need to recognise the key values that motivate you; to identify whether these values are being met; to learn how values influence your decisions and to develop a better self-awareness. Only then can you truly understand what you really want and how to obtain it.

Think about what really matters to you? Consider examples of events that have made you happy and made you sad. What about stressed and calm? If you really had no money concerns whatsoever, what would you do with your life, and why?

Ask your friends and family to describe you. What kind of person do they think you are? And what do they think are your strengths, weaknesses and interests?

Of course we have to live in the real world, and that usually means adding a large dose of practicality to our dreams – the bills still need paying after all. But we also owe it to ourselves to live happy and fulfilled lives.

Understanding your strengths and weaknesses

It is important to understand your strengths and your weaknesses. Not only might this help you choose a suitable future career, it will also identify areas that you need to work on.

How would you characterise your working style? What is your capacity to work under pressure? What kind of personality do you have? What are your communication skills like? Are you a confident person, or a bit shy? Are you creative? What about your social and technical skills?

Try writing a list of questions like this and then write down your answers (e.g. a SWOT analysis). Then ask your family and friends the same questions – and compare the answers.

Assessing your skills

Consider what skills, as a professional sportsperson, you have that potential employers might be interested in.

Professional sportspeople are a versatile crowd. Not only can they perform on the field, but they have boundless enthusiasm, ideas, flare and skill – qualities that are valuable to the business world.

Employers want employees who are committed, hard-working, are able to make decisions under pressure and are driven to succeed. It is virtually impossible to be successful as a professional sportsperson without having these qualities in abundance.

You have gained unique experience within a highly competitive environment.

You are highly motivated and have an appetite for success.

You will be committed to add to the success of your employer's business.

You have unique experience which can inspire other employees.

Having you on board would be good PR for your employer.

Bottom line – professional sportspeople have a lot of skills that employers value highly (and are often lacking within their non-sporting workforce).

GETTING QUALIFIED

Qualifications are usually a pre-requisite for most jobs and mandatory for anything skilled, so if you are still at school, college or university, don't ignore your education.

Maths and English are core subjects and employers will generally want candidates to have these. Sport may be easier and more exciting, but those exams will come in useful even if you don't end up using the specific subject skills directly.

Dave Butler, American Basketball – now Global Director of Dimensional Fund Advisers

"Always study something else – something you are interested in and enjoy. Because however hard it may be to envisage right now, your sports career will end."

If you have finished formal education then think about taking some part-time courses to either bulk-up or modernise your existing qualifications. Consider something that you might be interested in doing for a living one day – actually finding out more about it may spur on this interest, or perhaps convince you to think of an alternative.

Gaining experience

Up-to-date, relevant qualifications are always going to be useful, especially in an increasingly competitive marketplace. But experience is also valuable, especially for someone who may never have held down a "normal" job. And this can be virtually anything from helping out at local clubs, speaking at events, or working with associations and charities. Prospective employers are always looking for people who will put themselves out and make the effort to go that extra mile.

Look for companies who:

- Are interested in accessing an alternative talent pool.
- Can offer internship or seasonal work placement that might one day turn into a permanent opportunity.

MEET THE BUSINESS COMMUNITY

Many associations run business networking events, where pros can meet members of the local business community – and they you.

Such events offer a great opportunity to mingle with leading figures from all areas of business and find out more about life in the "normal" working world. You can discover more about possible career choices and get advice as to what qualifications and experience you might need. You might also get the odd offer of work experience, or advice from a successful businessman about setting up your own business.

But you don't have to wait for organised networking events; there are lots of opportunities for you to meet people who could be of benefit to you. The expertise, knowledge and contacts you can develop this way can be invaluable and will put you in a much stronger position when it comes time to leave sport.

Get in contact with your local Chamber of Commerce and ask someone about events in your area. Speak to local firms of solicitors and accountants – many of them run free seminars which draw people from across the business spectrum. There are always networking events being run by local firms (especially professional firms – accountants, lawyers, financial advisers), as well as those run by specialist networking firms.

The idea is not to worry too much about what business the host might be in, or what the topic of the seminar is. The aim is to get in the same room as people who might be of benefit to you. I have lost count of the number of times I have gained a valuable contact, or useful bit of information, from an event I was sure would be a waste of time.

Proper planning will certainly help you get the most out of any meeting. It is very easy to get side-tracked at these type of events – and drawn into conversations that, whilst might be of interest to the other party, are of little value to you.

Get hold of a list of attendees before you go and highlight the people you want to speak to. Make a list of objectives and SMART goals that you want to achieve. Focus on accomplishing these things and you will leave having made real, tangible progress.

The likelihood is that you will attend a few unproductive meetings, but if you speak to other attendees they will probably be able to suggest events that might be more suitable.

Using your name and fame

People want to meet professional sportspeople, so use this to your advantage. Think about who could be of benefit to you and approach them. If you are open, honest and upfront, most people will be more than willing to help you.

Preparing yourself for the workplace

Seek help making the right career choices and assistance in marketing yourself more effectively.

Your professional association is bound to know people who can advise you about recruitment and provide all sorts of career coaching. They will probably also have contacts within the local business community – businesses that may well be interested in employing sportspeople. There are also several recruitment agencies that are specifically focused on finding careers across all sectors for professional sportspeople.

CV AND APPLICATION LETTER WRITING

In such a competitive market it is vital that your CV and application letter accurately reflect your unique selling points.

Having a good CV is essential as it is often the only thing a prospective employer sees before making a decision about you – if it doesn't immediately impress, there are usually plenty more in the pile.

You need to ensure your CV makes the right impression and that it suits the job you are applying for. The style of your application letter needs to be correct – and both documents need to be individual and focus on *your* strengths and achievements. Including a professionally taken photo (not amateur) of yourself can help the reader connect with you on a personal level.

Experts suggest there are some basic rules on how a CV should be written and the information that should be included.

Overall, a CV should be neat and typed if possible. Most libraries now have public computers, if you do not have your own.

It should also be short, usually no more than two sides of A4.

It should be positive, stressing achievements and strengths, and make a good impression in a clear and positive way.

The basic format for a CV includes:

- Personal details, including name, address, phone number, email address and possibly any professional social media presence. You no longer need to include your date of birth, owing to age discrimination rules.

- Career history, starting with your most recent job first. Include dates and temporary or voluntary jobs if appropriate.
- A personal profile which sells yourself and your qualities, tailored towards the job you are applying for.
- Achievements from previous jobs that are relevant.
- Qualifications and training from previous jobs, with the most recent first.
- Interests, if they are relevant, and especially if the skills or teamwork concerned are relevant for the job.
- Any extra information, such as reasons for a career change or reasons for gaps in career history, such as caring duties.
- References, ideally two or more and including a recent employer.

A straightforward font and formatting is required – and the spelling must be checked and checked again. Poor spelling is the quickest way of getting a rejection.

Check five or six adverts for a particular job and then use the common requirements to mould your CV. It needs to be a very targeted document. Do some research so you understand what employers are looking for.

There is a lot of help and advice on CV writing available on the web and your professional association will undoubtedly have contacts who can help you.

The Department for Work and Pensions has a "Writing a CV" factsheet you can download from: http://www.dwp.gov.uk/docs/jobkit-cv-writing.pdf

Interview training

When you have never experienced it, the commercial world can be a daunting place. But any nerves you might have can be effectively managed with the right advice and coaching.

Tips and practical interview work e.g. role play, can help you prepare for interviews and ensure you promote the right image. Practising skills such as effective communication and body language can also ensure you are properly prepared. Again, your professional association will have contacts who can help you with all aspects of your post-sport career planning.

Meeting preparation

Whether you are going for an interview, or just meeting someone at a networking event, you have one chance to make a good impression.

- Preparation – is key, so think about what you are doing, why and what you would like the outcome to be.
- Find out about the company you are meeting e.g. look at their website.
- Have it clear in your mind what you can offer them.
- Arrive early – leave enough time so you don't have to rush and can relax and get your mind right when you get there.
- Need anything? Check you have it before you leave.
- Reminders – write key pointers on a card and keep it in your pocket. You can then sneak a quick look to remind yourself about key goals.
- Best clothes – wear clothes that make you look and feel good.
- Create first and last impressions – they are the ones people remember most.
- Build rapport – make an effort to get along and make a connection.
- Take three deep breaths – a couple of minutes before you go in.
- Recall a time you felt fantastic – and keep that in your mind.
- Go for it.

Recruitment firms

There are firms who will personally market your skills to companies that suit your talents and style of working. Several specialise in professional sportspeople – often run by ex-pros.

They can help you with all aspects of career planning, preparation and recruitment. Often they will help with preparation before each interview and can even handle salary negotiations. The goal is to make your transition from sport to employment as painless and stress free as possible.

Support from professional associations

Virtually every association now provides access to an excellent array of advice and guidance covering all aspects of post-sport career planning. In fact, they often see this as one of their most important roles.

They are keen to encourage as many members as possible to undertake suitable academic/vocational qualifications to develop their career prospects – both within and outside sport. Practical support includes offering information, advice and even grants towards courses leading to a recognised qualification.

One important point many associations make to their athletes is that:

"Learning need not only provide second career options but can also be part of a self-development programme."

They recognise that some pros can be reluctant to embark on courses because of the time commitment required. In response, many are arranging short taster courses in a range of topics which make learning interesting and accessible.

They are also making a huge effort to be a visible, approachable presence within clubs on a regular basis. Their hope is that this will make pros feel more comfortable discussing or enquiring about any courses or personal development programmes – encouraging a greater take up of the training and learning opportunities on offer.

STARTING YOUR OWN BUSINESS

Elite athletes have many of the skills that self-employed people need – focus, commitment, dedication, a good work ethic etc. However, that doesn't automatically mean that you will succeed if you set up your own business.

Just because you might be good at something e.g. physiotherapy, and are willing to work really hard, does not automatically mean that you will enjoy success. It is likely that you will need to acquire and master many new skills if you are thinking about setting up on your own.

As any self-employed person will tell you, there is a lot more to running a business than just providing the headline business service. A lot of your time will be spent doing other things – tasks that need to be done for the business just to operate, let alone be profitable.

If you are thinking about setting up your own business then you need to have a plan – even if it is written on a single sheet of paper. It doesn't have to run into pages, but there is something about the act of writing down what you are trying to do that really helps you gain clarity of purpose. It makes you think about things in detail; it will certainly help to highlight the things you need to do and also some of the challenges and issues that you will need to address. And, as you are likely to be asking people for help in certain areas, being able to give them a written plan will provide them with the information they need to help you.

One of the most important issues you need to sort out is the business finances. At the end of the day, there is no point pouring your heart and soul (and money) into a business if it is never likely to be profitable enough. Getting a good accountant on board early will be of huge help, as they can advise and guide you and help you develop your business plan.

But there simply is no substitute for having "been there, done that", so get as much input and advice from experienced and successful business people as you can. Talk to friends and family members who run their own businesses; work in similar businesses to the one you are thinking of setting up; and even contact people at local companies – most people are more than willing to help, even if they potentially are your competition.

Making use of other people's experience can help you by highlighting the main and most important issues that you need to address. It can minimise mistakes, save you from going down time-consuming and costly "blind alleys" and ensure that you address things before they become problems.

Perhaps the biggest reason for seeking advice is to find out what you don't know. Sometimes lessons are easy and cheap to learn, but other times they can be costly and game-changing.

So, get as much advice as you can whilst you are thinking about and planning your business venture. And even once you think you have got it all sorted out and ready to go, go back and ask your accountant and business contacts to give it a final look over and let you know what they think.

Remember, a great many new businesses fail within the first few years. The outcome for a lot of them could have been much different if they had just done their homework properly beforehand.

INVESTING IN SOMEONE ELSE'S BUSINESS

You have probably heard stories about (often retired) pros who have invested in businesses that subsequently failed – taking a great chunk of their savings with it. It is surprising just how often this happens, and to some of the most intelligent people – so have this reality firmly in your mind if you ever consider investing in someone else's business.
That is not to say that many pros haven't invested successfully in businesses – there are many who have, and it can work out well for both parties.

Pros are often approached because they have the cash available for investment, but it can also be because the business believes it could benefit from their fame, contacts and/or skills.

Being asked to invest in someone's business can be an exciting and potentially attractive option. But it can also be a difficult and dangerous position to find yourself in, especially if the business is owned by a family member, friend or local business acquaintance.

The first question you should ask yourself is: "Do I have any experience and/or expertise with this kind of business?" A lot of the time the answer will be "No", and this should be your first warning sign. Not because it means you shouldn't get involved, but because you shouldn't get involved until the proposal has been fully vetted by someone independent who does have the necessary experience and expertise to advise you properly.

Where is the business plan? Has it been signed-off by an accountant? Has the bank agreed to provide it with banking and credit facilities?

Many failed business ventures have started off sounding like sure-fire winners – real money makers. But in business many things can turn a seemingly good idea into a mire of stress and aggravation that just sucks up money like a sponge.

A good, independent business adviser (accountant or business owner/adviser) will look at an investment opportunity for you objectively and dispassionately. They will ask lots of questions in order to get to the heart of the proposal and to evaluate its validity and attractiveness.

- Is the business really worth what they say it is?
- Is it already successful without you?
- Do the owners/managers have a proven track record?
- Why do they need your money and what difference will it make to profitability and business value?
- Why can't/don't they get the money from a bank?
- What do they expect from you apart from cash? Can you do this?
- What have you really got to lose, apart from money?

You also need to consider the liquidity of any investment. It is likely that you won't just be able to pull your money out if you change your mind, or fall out with the other business owners. In fact, getting out at all might not be possible without incurring a large penalty or putting the business itself at risk.

Investing in someone else's business ultimately means relying on the skills and business acumen of others (and their honesty, ethics, morals, drive, goals, motivations etc). Don't ever go into it just because you think you know, or like that person and always get an independent expert to review the deal before committing.

MAKING A PASSIVE INVESTMENT

Many of the failed deals I know of have been "passive" business investments i.e. the pro invested money in the business, but that was about all – they had no real day-to-day involvement. In some cases the pro took a large share of the financial risk, whilst the other party's contribution was more in the way of coming up with the business concept and providing the skills, labour and know-how.

Now, investing money in a business and doing nothing to earn an income (and hopefully seeing the value of your capital rise), does sound like the perfect arrangement. However, the reality is that you are placing your money and your future completely in the hands of someone else and that is very risky.

As you won't know first-hand what is actually happening "on the shop floor" of the business, you will be completely reliant on someone else telling you. This puts you in a very precarious and vulnerable position. Many of the disasters that I know about involved family and friends – people the pro thought they could rely on to keep them informed and treat them fairly.

If you are ever considering making a business investment then you need to seek professional advice and part of that will be about how you protect yourself and your money in the event something goes wrong. This is especially critical if you are going to have little, or no involvement in the business itself.

What are your partners putting up as collateral/security – their savings and/or houses? Can you get some or all of your money out – under what circumstances?

GOING INTO BUSINESS WITH A FRIEND OR FAMILY MEMBER

I have already mentioned my reservations about mixing business with family and friends. This is not because I think this is always a bad idea; on the contrary, some of the most successful and enjoyable business ventures are those where friends and family work together. It is more that working with people you care about brings emotion into the business environment – and that can lead you to making decisions you wouldn't do otherwise.

The tendency when working with friends and family can be to keep things informal – in fact, it can feel "wrong" to be overly formal or prescriptive. People sometimes worry that acting "business-like" might offend, or cause tension and mistrust.

The problem is that just because you might be working with a friend or member of your family does not mean your business venture will succeed. It does not mean that you share the same attitudes and values about money and business. It does not mean that you won't fall out, or find yourself wanting to go in different directions at some point.

It is easy to assume that we all feel the same way about things but that is simply not the case – money especially is a very emotional subject. And even the simplest of misunderstandings can cause real problems and ruin relationships.

Talk about the business; your feelings about specific issues that might be important to you; and your hopes and expectations for the future. You need to ensure you are both on the same wavelength, or if you are not, that this fact is highlighted and addressed before you proceed. Glossing over or ignoring issues can lead to misunderstanding, resentment and frustration later on.

It is both realistic and very necessary to discuss money management openly and honestly.

Don't ever agree to anything until you have done your due diligence properly – don't be bullied or hurried. Make it clear from the outset that you will not make any decisions until you, and your advisers have looked at the proposal fully. If you make your position clear early on, then there is less chance you will feel emotional pressure to act.

Always get a second opinion – from an independent business professional.

JOINING A FRANCHISE

Rather than start your own business from scratch you could consider a franchise. This gives you the self-employed route but with the comfort of a tried and tested business model.

The most familiar form of franchising is "Business Format Franchising", which is the granting of a licence by one person (the franchisor) to another (the franchisee), that entitles the franchisee to trade as their own business, under the brand of the franchisor – following a proven business format.

As part of the deal the franchisee gets everything they need to establish their business – including training on all aspects of the business operation, so no previous experience is necessary. Ongoing support is also provided.

Providing you choose a good franchise, you will stand a very good chance of making it a success.

The key findings of the 2011 *(based on 2010 figures)* NatWest/BFA franchise survey:

- Estimated annual turnover of the business format franchise sector was £12.4 billion.
- The number of active franchises was 897.
- The average outlay for setting up a franchise was £81,900.
- Only 3.1% of franchises closed due to financial failure.
- 90% of franchises were profitable.
- The average starting age of a franchisee was 39.
- The average time a franchisee had been running their business was 8.4 years (and rising).

There are clear advantages to joining a franchise:

- You don't have to come up with a new idea – someone else has had it and proved it works.
- Larger, well-established franchise businesses will often have national advertising campaigns and a solid trading name.

- Good franchise businesses will offer comprehensive training programmes in sales and other important business skills.
- Good franchise businesses can also help secure funding for your investment as well as, for example, discounted bulk purchases for outlets when you are in operation.
- If customers are aware that you are running a franchise business, they will understand that you offer the best possible value for money and a consistent quality of service – although you run your 'own show', you are part of a much larger organisation.

For many people, the reason they don't consider a franchise (apart from their lack of general knowledge about them), is that they struggle to raise the money needed to buy one. Plus, most businesses take some time to get going and the income from a franchise may be depressed during its early years *(2011 NatWest/BFA survey – 28% of franchises reported losses in their first 2 years of trading).* But if you have been prudent during your playing career this may not be such a problem for you.

There are advantages and disadvantages to franchising and many considerations to make. You certainly need to think about this option carefully and take professional advice before making any decisions.

The British Franchise Association website contains lots of useful information if you want to find out more: http://www.thebfa.org/join-a-franchise

You could also visit one of the 3 main BFA approved franchise shows each year – London, Birmingham and Manchester.

WHAT IF YOU HAVE NO IDEA WHAT YOU WANT TO DO?

Some people will have no idea of what they want to do once their sporting career is over. Others don't care – or feel planning for their next career is not a priority for them right now.

The simple fact is that if you are not motivated to do something, nothing I can say will change your mind. But if this is the case, you do need to be honest about why.

If your career ended today, what would you do? It could happen.

Do you have the money, skills, education, experience, knowledge, and contacts to get a job that you would find fulfilling and would pay the bills?

If the answer is no, you should be doing something. Even if you don't have a clue what you want to end up doing, some preparation is better than none.

If you don't do "anything", how can you expect your current prospects to improve? It is highly unlikely that something will happen that will solve your dilemma overnight. If you don't try and help yourself, no-one else is going to!

> *"The definition of insanity is doing the same thing* (in this case – nothing), *over and over and expecting different results."*

Employers will always value experience and qualifications, even if they aren't necessarily in their field. In fact, many employers prefer applicants who have experience and qualifications from other areas, as it brings a fresh perspective. Learning can also be a journey of self-development, as well useful preparation for your next career.

Why not consider franchising? Have a look at what franchise opportunities are available (www.thebfa.org), and perhaps visit one of the BFA shows (London, Birmingham and Manchester.) At the very least, by looking at the diverse range of businesses that are out there *(over 900 to choose from!)* you might get some ideas about things you want to do – or at least tick off a few you definitely don't want to do. In either event, you would have made some progress.

CAN'T OR WON'T LET GO?

Financial pressures can force pros to continue competing – potentially longer than their performance warrants. This can be embarrassing for the pro concerned, when he/she just can't cut it with the youngsters any more.

Don't end up in the position where you need to keep going just to pay the bills. Get your finances organised early on in your professional career.

Some pros won't quit and this is a potentially more serious issue. Clinging on to a life that you know and love is understandable, but beyond a certain point it is not healthy.

Choosing when to quit is a highly personal decision and one that most pros think about a great deal towards the end of their careers. But if you have your finances in order, and your next career planned, at least you can make that decision on your own terms.

DEALING WITH ANXIETY AND DEPRESSION

It is important for all sports pros and their families to know how to access help if the need should arise.

The life of a professional sportsperson can be addictive and anxiety, depression and self-harm are understandably widespread issues.

Most associations are now extremely good at educating members, both current and past, to help them identify crucial warning signs and explain how they can get help.

Many high-profile sporting sufferers have done their bit by highlighting and thus de-stigmatising these issues. Many run sessions explaining how to recognise your feelings, your state of mind and how to reach for help, or accept offers of help.

If you have any concerns, don't be too proud to seek help. Your professional association probably has a great support system in place to help you through tough times – many offering full clinical and psychological support in conjunction with confidential helplines and access to benevolent funds. Speak to your association representative.

CONCLUSIONS

Your sporting career is likely to be short, which means that you need to plan for the next stage of your life well in advance.

Get your finances in order now, because you may well be reliant on them to maintain your lifestyle in future.

Get into good money habits and automate as much of your financial planning as possible – make life simple.

Review your finances on a regular basis; at least annually – and also whenever major changes occur in your life.

Start preparing for your post-sport career. Think about how you can build bridges between your current career and your next one.

Analyse your strengths, weaknesses, likes and dislikes etc. Get to know yourself – ask friends and family for their input.

Consider what qualifications might help you to achieve your career goals. Look at general qualifications if you are not sure what you want to do.

Gain as much work experience as you can – even if it is not within your chosen field.

Get out and meet people from the business community. Explore what opportunities might exist and how you can take advantage of them.

Your professional association will be able to provide lots of help and advice – so make the most of this valuable resource.

If you are thinking about starting your own business, get professional help and advice. Planning properly before you start will give you the best chance of success.

If you are considering investing in someone's business – beware. Get a suitable, independent business professional to help you with your due diligence.

No idea what you want to do? Do something! Any positive action that you can take now will help you in the future – even if it is not clear at the moment just how.

If you are having problems; either leaving sport, or with anxiety and/or depression, don't be too proud to seek help. There are lots of people who understand how you feel and are more than willing to provide you with support and advice.

EXERCISES – KEY IDEAS – ACTIVITIES

1. If you haven't got a Financial Plan – go back to the Preparation chapter and start to review the main aspects of your finances.

2. Set up automatic savings e.g. via direct debit; so that you put money aside regularly and without having to think about it.

3. Put a date in the diary to formally review your finances every year – perhaps when your professional life is less busy e.g. off season.

4. Start a list of possible post-sport careers – and write down beside each, the perceived pros and cons; as well as what you need to do to progress that option e.g. exams, speak to someone in that type of business etc.

5. Write down your strengths, weaknesses, likes and dislikes. Compare this list with your possible career options – does anything jump out at you?

6. What qualifications could you take that would help you with your post-sport career? If you are not sure what you might want to do; what general qualifications (e.g. Maths and English), would you find useful and/or interesting?

7. Meet as many people within the business community as you can. Build contacts and leverage these to help you towards your post-sport goals.

8. Contact someone at your professional association and ask them what they can do to help you. They probably have a lot of practical advice and support they can offer you.

9. If you are thinking about setting up your own business, or investing in someone else's, seek advice from an independent, business professional.

10. Even if you have no idea what you might want to do, that is no excuse for inaction. At least do "something" and you will probably find that the next step is much easier and clearer.

11. If you are having problems, then don't hesitate. Pick up the phone and ask for help.

NOTES

CLOSING REMARKS

This book is all about making the most of your current life – whilst also planning for the future.

The core theme has been good money management – because even if you find it boring, tedious or even baffling, you almost certainly don't find money unattractive – and more of it is undoubtedly what you will have if you get your finances organised properly.

And remember that your finances are very much like a car engine – they need tuning and on-going maintenance if they are to run effectively and efficiently.

But what we do is always going to be more important and more fulfilling than what we can buy. Your sporting career can provide you with an excellent springboard to the next stage of your life; but how successful that transition will be all depends on you – you need to work on it.

Whilst you may feel you don't have the time to do all these things (or perhaps even want to make the time), there is no doubt that a small investment now will pay huge dividends in the longer-term.

At the end of the day, it is the quality of your current and future life that is at stake.

With best wishes,

Darren Baker

DALAI LAMA'S "GOOD KARMA" ADVICE FOR LIFE

I thought I would leave you with something positive.

I saw this list in a paper many years ago, I duly cut it out, and it has been stuck on my office wall ever since. I hope you find something inspirational in these words too.

1. Realise that great love and great achievements involve great risk.

2. When you lose, don't lose the lesson.

3. Follow the three R's: Respect for self. Respect for others. Responsibility for your actions.

4. Remember that not getting what you want is often a stroke of luck.

5. Learn the rules so you know how to break them properly.

6. Don't let a little dispute injure a great relationship.

7. When you realise you've made a mistake, move to correct it immediately.

8. Spend some time alone every day.

9. Open your arms to change but don't let go of your values.

10. Remember that silence is sometimes the best answer.

11. Live a good, honourable life. Then when you get older and think back, you'll enjoy it a second time.

12. A loving atmosphere at home is the foundation of your life.

13. In disagreements with loved ones, deal only with the current situation. Don't bring up the past.

14. Share your knowledge. It is a way to achieve immortality.

15. Be gentle with the earth.

16. Once a year, go somewhere you've never been before.

17. Remember that the best relationship is one in which your love for each other exceeds your need for each other.

18. Judge your success by what you had to give up in order to get it.

DISCLAIMER AND LEGAL NOTICE

A GLOSSARY OF COMMON FINANCIAL TERMS

On a daily basis we get bombarded with financial terms and jargon. The following list is by no means comprehensive, but it will hopefully provide an explanation for some of the more common words used in the UK media.

A

AAA-rating: The best credit rating that can be given to a borrower's debts, indicating that the risk of a borrower defaulting is minuscule.

Administration: A rescue mechanism for UK companies in severe trouble. It allows them to continue as a going concern, under supervision, giving them the opportunity to try to work their way out of difficulty. A firm in administration cannot be wound up without permission from a court.

AGM: An annual general meeting, which companies hold each year for shareholders to vote on important issues such as dividend payments and appointments to the company's board of directors. If an emergency decision is needed – for example in the case of a takeover – a company may also call an exceptional general meeting of shareholders or EGM.

Assets: Things that provide income or some other value to their owner.

- Fixed assets (also known as long-term assets) are things that have a useful life of more than one year, for example buildings and machinery; there are also intangible fixed assets, like the good reputation of a company or brand.
- Current assets are the things that can easily be turned into cash and are expected to be sold or used up in the near future.

Austerity: Economic policy aimed at reducing a government's deficit (or borrowing). Austerity can be achieved through increases in government revenues – primarily via tax rises – and/or a reduction in government spending or future spending commitments.

B

Bailout: The financial rescue of a struggling borrower. A bailout can be achieved in various ways:

- providing loans to a borrower that markets will no longer lend to
- guaranteeing a borrower's debts
- guaranteeing the value of a borrower's risky assets
- providing help to absorb potential losses, such as in a bank recapitalisation

Bankruptcy: A legal process in which the assets of a borrower who cannot repay its debts – which can be an individual, a company or a bank – are valued, and possibly sold off (liquidated), in order to repay debts.

Where the borrower's assets are insufficient to repay its debts, the debts have to be written off. This means the lenders must accept that some of their loans will never be repaid, and the borrower is freed of its debts. Bankruptcy varies greatly from one country to another; some countries have laws that are very friendly to borrowers, while others are much more friendly to lenders.

Base rate: The key interest rate set by the Bank of England. It is the overnight interest rate that it charges to banks for lending to them. The base rate – and expectations about how the base rate will change in the future – directly affect the interest rates at which banks are willing to lend money in sterling.

Basis point: One hundred basis points make up a percentage point, so an interest rate cut of 25 basis points might take the rate, for example, from 3% to 2.75%.

BBA: The British Bankers' Association is an organisation representing the major banks in the UK – including foreign banks with a major presence in London. It is responsible for the daily Libor interest rate which determines the rate at which banks lend to each other.

Bear market: In a bear market, prices are falling and investors, fearing losses, tend to sell. This can create a self-sustaining downward spiral.

Bill: A debt security – or more simply an IOU. It is very similar to a bond, but has a maturity of less than one year when first issued.

Bond: A debt security, or more simply, an IOU. The bond states when a loan must be repaid and what interest the borrower (issuer) must pay to the holder. They can be issued by companies, banks or governments to raise money. Banks and investors buy and trade bonds.

BRIC: An acronym used to describe the fast-growing economies of Brazil, Russia, India and China.

Bull market: A bull market is one in which prices are generally rising and investor confidence is high.

C

Capital: For investors, it refers to their stock of wealth, which can be put to work in order to earn income. For companies, it typically refers to sources of financing such as newly issued shares. For banks, it refers to their ability to absorb losses in their accounts. Banks normally obtain capital either by issuing new shares, or by keeping hold of profits instead of paying them out as dividends. If a bank writes off a loss on one of its assets – for example, if it makes a loan that is not repaid – then the bank must also write off a corresponding amount of its capital. If a bank runs out of capital, then it is insolvent, meaning it does not have enough assets to repay its debts.

Capital adequacy ratio: A measure of a bank's ability to absorb losses. It is defined as the value of its capital divided by the value of risk-weighted assets (i.e. taking into account how risky they are). A low capital adequacy ratio suggests that a bank has a limited ability to absorb losses, given the amount and the riskiness of the loans it has made. A banking regulator – typically the central bank – sets a minimum capital adequacy ratio for the banks in each country, and an international minimum standard is set by the BIS. A bank that fails to meet this minimum standard must be recapitalised, for example by issuing new shares.

Collateralised debt obligations (CDOs): A financial structure that groups individual loans, bonds or other assets in a portfolio, which can then be traded. In theory, CDOs attract a stronger credit rating than individual assets due to the risk being more diversified. But as the performance of many assets fell during the financial crisis, the value of many CDOs was also reduced.

Commercial paper: Unsecured, short-term loans taken out by companies. The funds are typically used for working capital, rather than fixed assets such as a new building. The loans take the form of IOUs that can be bought and traded by banks and investors, similar to bonds.

Commodities: Commodities are products that, in their basic form, are all the same so it makes little difference from whom you buy them. That means that they can have a common market price. You would be unlikely to pay more for iron ore just because it came from a particular mine, for example. Contracts to buy and sell commodities usually specify minimum common standards, such as the form and purity of the product, and where and when it must be delivered. The commodities markets range from soft commodities such as sugar, cotton and pork bellies to industrial metals such as iron and zinc.

Core inflation: A measure of CPI inflation that strips out more volatile items (typically food and energy prices). The core inflation rate is watched closely by central bankers, as it tends to give a clearer indication of long-term inflation trends.

Correction (market): A short-term drop in stock market prices. The term comes from the notion that, when this happens, overpriced or under-priced stocks are returning to their "correct" values.

CPI: The Consumer Prices Index is a measure of the price of a bundle of goods and services from across the economy. It is the most common measure used to identify inflation in a country. CPI is used as the target measure of inflation by the Bank of England and the ECB.

Credit crunch: A situation where banks and other lenders all cut back their lending at the same time, because of widespread fears about the ability of borrowers to repay. If heavily-indebted borrowers are cut off from new lending, they may find it impossible to repay existing debts. Reduced lending also slows down economic growth, which also makes it harder for all businesses to repay their debts.

Credit rating: The assessment given to debts and borrowers by a ratings *agency* according to their safety from an investment standpoint – based on their creditworthiness, or the ability of the company or government that is borrowing to repay. Ratings range from *AAA*, the safest, down to D, a company that has already defaulted. Ratings of BBB – or higher are considered "investment grade". Below that level, they are considered "speculative grade" or more colloquially as junk.

D

Dead cat bounce: A phrase long used on trading floors to describe the small rebound in market prices typically seen following a sharp fall.

Debt restructuring: A situation in which a borrower renegotiates the terms of its debts, usually in order to reduce short-term debt repayments and to increase the amount of time it has to repay them. If lenders do not agree to the change in repayment terms, or if the restructuring results in an obvious loss to lenders, then it is generally considered a default by the borrower. However, restructuring can also occur through a debt swap – a voluntary agreement by lenders to switch existing debts for new debts with easier repayment terms – in which case it can be very hard to determine whether the restructuring counts as a default.

Default: Strictly speaking, a default occurs when a borrower has broken the terms of a loan or other debt, for example if a borrower misses a payment. The term is also loosely used to mean any situation that makes it clear that a borrower can no longer repay its debts in full, such as bankruptcy or a debt restructuring. A default can have a number of important implications. If a borrower is in default on any one debt, then all of its lenders may be able to demand that the borrower immediately repay them. Lenders may also be required to write off their losses on the loans they have made.

Deficit: The amount by which spending exceeds income over the course of a year. In the case of trade, it refers to exports minus imports. In the case of the government budget, it equals the amount the government needs to borrow during the year to fund its spending. The government's "primary" deficit means the amount it needs to borrow to cover general government expenditure, excluding interest payments on debts. The primary deficit therefore indicates whether a government will run out of cash if it is no longer able to borrow and decides to stop repaying its debts.

Deflation: Negative inflation – that is, when the prices of goods and services across the whole economy are falling on average.

Deleveraging: A process whereby borrowers reduce their debt loads. Primarily this occurs by repaying debts. It can also occur by bankruptcies and debt defaults, or by the borrowers increasing their incomes, meaning that their existing debt loads become more manageable. Western economies are experiencing widespread deleveraging, a process associated with weak economic growth that is expected to last years. Households are deleveraging by repaying mortgage and credit card debts. Banks are deleveraging by cutting back on lending. Governments are also beginning to deleverage via austerity programmes – cutting spending and increasing taxation.

Derivative: A financial contract which provides a way of investing in a particular product without having to own it directly. For example, a stock market futures contract allows investors to make bets on the value of a stock market index such as the FTSE 100 without having to buy or sell any shares. The value of a derivative can depend on anything from the price of coffee to interest rates or what the weather is like. Credit derivatives such as credit default swaps depend on the ability of a borrower to repay its debts. Derivatives allow investors and banks to hedge their risks, or to speculate on markets. Futures, forwards, swaps and options are all types of derivatives.

Dividends: An income payment by a company to its shareholders usually linked to its profits.

Double-dip recession: A recession that experiences a limited recovery then dips back into recession. The exact definition is unclear, as the definition of what counts as a recession varies between countries. A widely-accepted definition is one where the initial recovery fails to take total economic output back up to the peak seen before the recession began.

E

ECB: The European Central Bank is the central bank responsible for monetary policy in the Eurozone. It is headquartered in Frankfurt and has a mandate to ensure price stability – which is interpreted as an inflation rate of no more than 2% per year.

ESM: The European Stability Mechanism is a 500bn-euro rescue fund that replaced the

EFSF and the EFSM from June 2013. Unlike the EFSF, the ESM is a permanent bail-out arrangement for the Eurozone. Unlike the EFSM, the ESM will only be backed by members of the Eurozone, and not by other European Union members such as the UK.

EFSF: The European Financial Stability Facility is currently a temporary fund worth up to 440bn euros set up by the Eurozone in May 2010. Following a previous bail-out of Greece, the EFSF was originally intended to help other struggling Eurozone governments, and has since provided rescue loans to the Irish Republic and Portugal. More recently, the Eurozone agreed to broaden the EFSF's mandate, for example by allowing it to support banks.

EFSM: The European Financial Stability Mechanism is 60bn euros of money pledged by the member governments of the European Union, including 7.5bn euros pledged by the UK. The EFSM has been used to loan money to the Irish Republic and Portugal. It will be replaced by the ESM from 2013.

Equity: The value of a business or investment after subtracting any debts owed by it. The equity in a company is the value of all its shares. In a house, your equity is the amount your house is worth minus the amount of mortgage debt that is outstanding on it.

Eurobond: A term increasingly used for the idea of a common, jointly-guaranteed bond of the Eurozone governments. It has been mooted as a solution to the Eurozone debt crisis, as it would prevent markets from differentiating between the creditworthiness of different government borrowers. Confusingly and quite separately, "Eurobond" also refers to a bond issued in a country which isn't denominated in that country's currency. For example, this is used to refer to bonds in US dollars issued in Europe.

Eurozone: The 17 countries that share the euro.

F

Federal Reserve: The US central bank.

Financial Policy Committee: A new committee at the Bank of England set up in 2010-11 in response to the financial crisis. It has overall responsibility for ensuring major risks do not build up within the UK financial system.

Financial transaction tax: See Tobin tax.

Fiscal policy: The government's borrowing, spending and taxation decisions. If a government is worried that it is borrowing too much, it can engage in austerity; raising taxes and/or cutting spending. Alternatively, if a government is afraid that the economy is going into recession it can engage in fiscal stimulus, which can include cutting taxes, raising spending and/or raising borrowing.

FTSE 100: An index of the 100 companies listed on the London Stock Exchange with the biggest market value. The index is revised every three months.

Fundamentals: Fundamentals determine a company, currency or security's value in the long-term. A company's fundamentals include its assets, debt, revenue, earnings and growth.

Futures: A futures contract is an agreement to buy or sell a commodity at a predetermined date and price. It could be used to hedge or to speculate on the price of the commodity. Futures contracts are a type of derivative, and are traded on an exchange.

G

G7: The group of seven major industrialised economies, comprising the US, UK, France, Germany, Italy, Canada and Japan.

G8: The G7 plus Russia.

G20; The G8 plus developing countries that play an important role in the global economy, such as China, India, Brazil and Saudi Arabia. It gained in significance after leaders agreed how to tackle the 2008-09 financial crisis and recession at G20 gatherings.

GDP: Gross Domestic Product. A measure of economic activity in a country, namely of all the services and goods produced in a year. There are three main ways of calculating GDP – through output, through income and through expenditure.

H

Haircut: A reduction in the value of a troubled borrower's debts, imposed on, or agreed with, its lenders as part of a debt restructuring.

Hedge fund: A private investment fund which uses a range of sophisticated strategies to maximise returns including hedging, leveraging and derivatives trading. Authorities around the world are working on ways to regulate them.

Hedging: Making an investment to reduce the risk of price fluctuations to the value of an asset. Airlines often hedge against rising oil prices by agreeing in advance to buy their fuel at a set price. In this case, a rise in price would not harm them – but nor would they benefit from any falls.

I

IMF: The International Monetary Fund is an organisation set up after World War II to provide financial assistance to governments. Since the 1980s, the IMF has been most active in providing rescue loans to the governments of developing countries that run into debt problems. Since the financial crisis, the IMF has also provided rescue loans, alongside the European Union governments and the ECB, to Greece, the Irish Republic and Portugal. The IMF is traditionally – and of late controversially – headed by a European.

Impairment charge: The amount written off by a company when it realises that it has valued an asset more highly than it is actually worth.

Independent Commission on Banking: A commission chaired by economist Sir John Vickers set up in 2010 by the UK government in order to make recommendations on how to reform the banking system. The commission reported back in September 2011, and called for:

- a ring-fence, to separate and safeguard the activities of banks that were deemed essential to the UK economy
- measures to increase the transparency of bank accounts and competition among banks, including the creation of a new major High Street bank
- much higher capital requirements for the big banks so that they can better absorb future losses

Inflation: The upward price movement of goods and services.

Insolvency: A situation in which the value of a borrower's *assets* is not enough to repay all of its debts. If a borrower can be shown to be insolvent, it normally means they can be declared *bankrupt* by a court.

Investment bank: Investment banks provide financial services for governments, companies or extremely rich individuals. They differ from commercial banks where you have your savings or your mortgage. Traditionally investment banks provided underwriting, and financial advice on mergers and acquisitions, and how to raise money in the financial markets. The term is also commonly used to describe the more risky activities typically undertaken by such firms, including trading directly in financial markets for their own account.

J

Junk bond: A bond with a credit rating of BB+ or lower. These debts are considered very risky by the ratings agencies. Typically the bonds are traded in markets at a price that offers a very high yield (return to investors) as compensation for the higher risk of default.

K

Keynesian economics: The economic theories of John Maynard Keynes. In modern political parlance, the belief that the state can directly stimulate demand in a stagnating economy, for instance, by borrowing money to spend on public works projects such as roads, schools and hospitals.

L

Leverage: Leverage, or gearing, means using debt to supplement investment. The more you borrow on top of the funds (or equity) you already have, the more highly leveraged you are. Leverage can increase both gains and losses. Deleveraging means reducing the amount you are borrowing.

Liability: A debt or other form of payment obligation, listed in a company's accounts.

Libor: London Inter-Bank Offered Rate. The rate at which banks in London lend money to each other for the short-term in a particular currency. A new Libor rate is calculated every morning by financial data firm Thomson Reuters based on interest rates provided by members of the British Bankers Association.

Limited liability: Confines an investor's loss in a business to the amount of *capital* they invested. If a person invests £100,000 in a company and it goes under, they will lose only their investment and not more.

Liquidation: A process in which assets are sold off for cash. Liquidation is often the outcome for a company deemed irretrievably loss-making. In that case, its assets are sold off individually, and the cash proceeds are used to repay its lenders. In liquidation, a company's lenders and other claimants are given an order of priority. Usually the tax authorities are the first to be paid, while the company's shareholders are the last, and typically receiving nothing.

Liquidity: How easy something is to convert into cash. Your current account, for example, is more liquid than your house. If you needed to sell your house quickly to pay bills you would have to drop the price substantially to get a sale.

Liquidity crisis: A situation in which it suddenly becomes much more difficult for banks to obtain cash due to a general loss of confidence in the financial system. Investors (and, in the case of a bank run, even ordinary depositors) may withdraw their cash from banks, while banks may stop lending to each other, if they fear that some banks could go bust. Because most of a bank's money is tied up in loans, even a healthy bank can run out of cash and collapse in a liquidity crisis. Central banks usually respond to a liquidity crisis by acting as "lender of last resort" and providing emergency cash loans to the banks.

Liquidity trap: A situation described by economist John Maynard Keynes in which nervousness about the economy leads everybody to cut back on their spending and to hold cash, even if the cash earns no interest. The widespread fall in spending undermines the economy, which in turn makes households, banks and companies even more nervous about spending and investing their money. The problem becomes particularly intractable when – as in Japan over the last 20 years – the weak spending leads to falling prices, which creates a stronger incentive for people to hold onto their cash, and also makes debts more difficult to repay. In a liquidity trap, monetary policy can become useless, and Keynes said that the onus is on governments to increase their spending.

Loans-to-deposit ratio: For financial institutions, the sum of their loans divided by the sum of their deposits. It is used as a way of measuring a bank's vulnerability to the loss of confidence in a liquidity crisis. Deposits are typically guaranteed by the bank's government and are therefore considered a safer source of funding for the bank. Before the 2008 financial crisis, many banks became reliant on other sources of funding – meaning they had very high loan-to-deposit ratios. When these other sources of funding suddenly evaporated, the banks were left critically short of cash.

M

Monetary policy: The policies of the central bank. A central bank has an unlimited ability to create new money. This allows it to control the short-term interest rate, as well as to engage in unorthodox policies such as quantitative easing – printing money to buy up government debts and other assets. Monetary policy can be used to control inflation and to support economic growth.

Money markets: Global markets dealing in borrowing and lending on a short-term basis.

MPC: The Monetary Policy Committee of the Bank of England is responsible for setting short-term interest rates and other monetary policy in the UK, such as quantitative easing.

N

Nationalisation: The act of bringing an industry or assets such as land and property under state control.

Negative equity: Refers to a situation in which the value of your house is less than the amount of the mortgage that still has to be paid off.

O

Options; A type of derivative that gives an investor the right to buy (or to sell) something – anything from a share to a barrel of oil – at an agreed price and at an agreed time in the future. Options become much more valuable when markets are volatile, as they can be an insurance against price swings.

P

Ponzi scheme: Similar to a pyramid scheme, an enterprise where funds from new investors – instead of genuine profits – are used to pay high returns to current investors. Named after the Italian fraudster Charles Ponzi, such schemes are destined to collapse as soon as new investment tails off or significant numbers of investors simultaneously wish to withdraw funds.

Preference shares: A class of shares that usually do not offer voting rights, but do offer a superior type of dividend, paid ahead of dividends to ordinary shareholders. Preference shareholders often also have somewhat better protection when a company is liquidated.

Private equity fund: An investment fund that specialises in buying up troubled or undervalued companies, reorganising them, and then selling them off at a profit.

PPI: The Producer Prices Index, a measure of the wholesale prices at which factories and other producers are able to sell goods in an economy.

Profit warning: When a company issues a statement indicating that its profits will not be as high as it had expected.

Q

Quantitative easing: Central banks increase the supply of money by "printing" more. In practice, this may mean purchasing government bonds or other categories of assets, using the new money. Rather than physically printing more notes, the new money is typically issued in the form of a deposit at the central bank. The idea is to add more money into the system, which depresses the value of the currency, and to push up the value of the assets being bought and to lower longer-term interest rates, which encourages more borrowing and investment. Some economists fear that quantitative easing can lead to very high inflation in the long term.

R

Rating: The assessment given to debts and borrowers by a ratings agency according to their safety from an investment standpoint – based on their creditworthiness, or the ability of the company or government that is borrowing to repay. Ratings range from AAA, the safest, down to D, a company that has already defaulted. Ratings of BBB or higher are considered "investment grade". Below that level, they are considered "speculative grade" or more colloquially as junk.

Rating agency: A company responsible for issuing credit ratings. The major three rating agencies are Moody's, Standard and Poor's and Fitch.

Recapitalisation: To inject fresh equity into a firm or a bank, which can be used to absorb future losses and reduce the risk of insolvency. Typically this will happen via the firm issuing new shares. The cash raised can also be used to repay debts. In the case of a government recapitalising a bank, it results in the government owning a stake in the bank. In an extreme case, such as Royal Bank of Scotland, it can lead to nationalisation, where the government owns a majority of the bank.

Recession: A period of negative economic growth. In most parts of the world a recession is technically defined as two consecutive quarters of negative growth – when economic output falls. In the United States, a larger number of factors are taken into account, such as job creation and manufacturing activity. However, this means that a US recession can usually only be defined when it is already over.

Reserve currency: A currency that is widely held by foreign central banks around the world in their reserves. The US dollar is the pre-eminent reserve currency, but the euro, pound, yen and Swiss franc are also popular.

Reserves: Assets accumulated by a central bank, which typically comprise gold and foreign currency. Reserves are usually accumulated in order to help the central bank defend the value of the currency, particularly when its value is pegged to another foreign currency or to gold.

Retained earnings: Profits not paid out by a company as dividends and held back to be reinvested.

Rights issue: When a public company issues new shares to raise cash. The company might do this for a number or reasons – because it is running short of cash, because it wants to make an expensive investment or because it needs to be recapitalised. By putting more shares on the market, a company dilutes the value of its existing shares. It is called a "rights" issue, because existing shareholders have the first right to buy the new shares, thereby avoiding dilution of their existing shares.

Ring-fence: A recommendation of the UK's Independent Commission on Banking. Services provided by the banks that are deemed essential to the UK economy – such as customer accounts, payment transfers, lending to small and medium businesses – should be separated out from the banks' other, riskier activities. They would be placed in a separate subsidiary company in the bank, and provided with its own separate capital to absorb any losses. The ring-fenced business would also be banned from lending to or in other ways exposing itself to the risks of the rest of the bank – in particular its investment banking activities.

S

Securities lending: When one broker or dealer lends a security (such as a bond or a share) to another for a fee. This is the process that allows short selling.

Securitisation: Turning something into a security. For example, taking the debt from a number of mortgages and combining them to make a financial product, which can then be traded (see mortgage backed securities). Investors who buy these securities receive income when the original home-buyers make their mortgage payments.

Security: A contract that can be assigned a value and traded. It could be a share, a bond or a mortgage-backed security. Separately, the term "security" is also used to mean something that is pledged by a borrower when taking out a loan. For example, mortgages in the UK are usually secured on the borrower's home. This means that if the borrower cannot repay, the lender can seize the security – the home – and sell it in order to help repay the outstanding debt.

Short selling: A technique used by investors who think the price of an asset, such as shares or oil contracts, will fall. They borrow the asset from another investor and then sell it in the relevant market. The aim is to buy back the asset at a lower price and return it to its owner, pocketing the difference. Also known as shorting.

Spread (yield): The difference in the yield of two different bonds of approximately the same maturity, usually in the same currency. The spread is used as a measure of the market's perception of the difference in creditworthiness of two borrowers.

Stagflation: The dreaded combination of inflation and stagnation – an economy that is not growing while prices continue to rise. Most major western economies experienced stagflation during the 1970s.

Stimulus: Monetary policy or fiscal policy aimed at encouraging higher growth and/or inflation. This can include interest rate cuts, quantitative easing, tax cuts and spending increases.

Sub-prime mortgages: These carry a higher risk to the lender (and therefore tend to be at higher interest rates) because they are offered to people who have had financial problems or who have low or unpredictable incomes.

Swap: A derivative that involves an exchange of cash flows between two parties. For example, a bank may swap out of a fixed long-term interest rate into a variable short-term interest rate, or a company may swap a flow of income out of a foreign currency into their own currency.

T

Tobin tax: A tax on financial transactions, originally proposed by economist James Tobin as a levy on currency conversions. The tax is intended to discourage market speculators by making their activities uneconomic, and in this way, to increase stability in financial markets. The idea was originally pushed by former UK Prime Minister Gordon Brown in response to the financial crisis. More recently it has been formally proposed by the European Commission, with some suggesting the revenue could be used to tackle the financial crisis. It is now opposed by the current UK government, which argues that to be effective, the tax would need to be applied globally – not just in the EU – as most financial activities could quite easily be relocated to another country in order to avoid the tax.

Toxic debts: Debts that are very unlikely to be recovered from borrowers. Most lenders expect that some customers cannot repay; toxic debt describes a whole package of loans that are unlikely to be repaid. During the financial crisis, toxic debts were very hard to value or to sell, as the markets for them ceased to function. This greatly increased uncertainty about the financial health of the banks that owned much of these debts.

Troika: The term used to refer to the European Union, the European Central Bank and the International Monetary Fund – the three organisations charged with monitoring Greece's progress in carrying out austerity measures as a condition of bailout loans provided to it by the IMF and by other European governments. The bailout loans are being released in a number of tranches of cash, each of which must be approved by the troika's inspectors.

U

Underwriters: The financial institution pledging to purchase a certain number of newly-issued securities if they are not all bought by investors. The underwriter is typically an investment bank who arranges the new issue. The need for an underwriter can arise when a company makes a rights issue or a bond issue.

Unwind: To unwind a deal is to reverse it – to sell something that you have previously bought, or vice versa, or to cancel a derivative contract for an agreed payment. When administrators are called in to a bank, they must do the unwinding before creditors can get any money back.

V

Vickers Report: See Independent Commission on Banking.

W

Warrants: A document entitling the bearer to receive shares, usually at a stated price.

Working capital: A measure of a company's ability to make payments falling due in the next 12 months. It is calculated as the difference between the company's current assets (unsold inventories plus any cash expected to be received over the coming year) minus its current liabilities (what the company owes over the same period). A healthy company should have a positive working capital. A company with negative working capital can experience cashflow problems.

World Bank: Set up after World War II along with the IMF, the World Bank is mainly involved in financing development projects aimed at reducing world poverty. The World Bank is traditionally headed by an American, while the IMF is headed by a European. Like the IMF and OECD, the World Bank produces economic data and research, and comments on global economic policy.

Write-down: Reducing the book value of an asset, either to reflect a fall in its market value (see mark-to-market) or due to an impairment charge.

Y

Yield: The return to an investor from buying a bond implied by the bond's current market price. It also indicates the current cost of borrowing in the market for the bond issuer. As a bond's market price falls, its yield goes up, and vice versa. Yields can increase for a number of reasons. Yields for all bonds in a particular currency will rise if markets think that the central bank in that currency will raise short-term interest rates due to stronger growth or higher inflation. Yields for a particular borrower's bonds will rise if markets think there is a greater risk that the borrower will default.

Z

Can't think of any!

SOME USEFUL WEBSITES

The aim of this section is to provide a manageable selection of website addresses for further information. This list, therefore, does not seek to be exhaustive and, consequently, it may not list some sites that are relevant.

Yourfinancialcoach.co.uk
QED ProSports – Darren Baker's financial and investment consultancy business.
http://www.yourfinancialcoach.co.uk

Unbiased.co.uk
A site that allows you to source all sorts of professional advisers (investment, pension, mortgage, tax, property, insurance and business), by specialism, qualifications and area.
http://www.unbiased.co.uk/

Vouchedfor.co.uk
A search site purely for reasonably qualified financial advisers – many of whom display endorsements from their existing clients.
http://www.vouchedfor.co.uk/search-for-ifa

Institute of Financial Planning
The Institute of Financial Planning is the professional organisation of choice for some of the UK's leading advisers.
http://www.financialplanning.org.uk/directory

The Money Advice Service
Clear, unbiased money advice to help people make informed choices.
www.moneyadviceservice.org.uk
Tel: 0300 500 5000.

The Citizens Advice Bureau
Free, independent and confidential help with legal, money and other problems.
http://www.citizensadvice.org.uk/

The Pensions Regulator
Information about all aspects of pensions and retirement planning; plus links to lots of other useful sites and information sources.
http://www.thepensionsregulator.gov.uk/individuals.aspx

HMRC Self-Assessment
The official HMRC site that explains when you might need to complete a tax return and, if so, how to do it.
http://www.hmrc.gov.uk/sa/introduction.htm

HMRC
The main HMRC site that provides lots of information about all aspects of tax and state benefits e.g. tax credits and child benefit.
http://www.hmrc.gov.uk

British Franchise Association
Lots of useful information and advice about business franchising.
http://www.thebfa.org/Home

Connexions Direct
Information, advice and guidance service for young people.
www.connexions-direct.com

Directgov
Jobs, training and career opportunities, plus access to other public services.
www.direct.gov.uk

Merlin Helps Students
Student resource website.
www.merlinhelpsstudents.com/

Money Saving Expert
Not-for-profit site offering tips and tricks for financing study and other costs.
www.moneysavingexpert.com

National Careers Service
Local careers advice, job matching, psychometric testing.
https://nationalcareersservice.direct.gov.uk

Ofqual
The Register of Regulated Qualifications contains details of Recognised Awarding Organisations and Regulated Qualifications.
http://register.ofqual.gov.uk/

Open University
Degree programmes via supported open learning (distance learning).
http://www.open.ac.uk/

Student Finances
Government information on loans and grants for college/university.
http://www.direct.gov.uk/

Third Sector Jobs
Job vacancies within the charity, voluntary or not-for-profit sector.
http://jobs.thirdsector.co.uk/

UCAS
Central point for applying for full-time undergraduate courses.
http://www.ucas.com

ABOUT THE AUTHOR

Darren Baker
ACII APFS AIFP CFP

Darren has over 25 years' experience working as a financial planner; initially with a high street bank before becoming a director of a regional financial services and accountancy firm. Since 1997 he has run his own financial planning firm advising successful clients across the UK.

One of an elite group who hold both "Chartered Financial Planner" and "Certified Financial Planner" qualifications, Darren's extensive credentials cover a wide range of disciplines including investments, pensions, tax, financial planning, law and trusts.

A keen competitor, Darren likes to take part in various endurance/adventure, swimming and triathlon events – when not injured! A proud father of two, he is a Governor of the local Maths and Computing Academy and member of several business clubs.

Other interests, children's schedules permitting, include spending time with family and friends, travelling, diving, walking, cycling, wildlife, reading, gardening, live music, golf, most other sports and anything that is different and/or a challenge.

Darren's passions are his family, friends and getting the most out of life. His pet "soap box" topics are pessimists, the "herd mentality" and most adverts on TV.